D1218691

THE ENGLISH HEROIC PLAY

THE ENGLISH HEROIC PLAY

A CRITICAL DESCRIPTION OF THE RHYMED TRAGEDY OF THE RESTORATION

BY

LEWIS NATHANIEL CHASE

New York
RUSSELL & RUSSELL
1965

Columbia University

STUDIES IN COMPARATIVE LITERATURE

FIRST PUBLISHED IN 1903
REISSUED, 1965, BY RUSSELL & RUSSELL, INC.
L.C. CATALOG CARD NO: 65—13995
PRINTED IN THE UNITED STATES OF AMERICA

PREFACE

THIS essay was submitted in partial fulfilment of the requirements for the degree of Doctor of Philosophy at Columbia University. A study of the English tragic drama of the latter half of the seventeenth century falls naturally into three parts: first, a critical survey of the plays with the object of determining the type; second, an inquiry into foreign origins and parallels; third, a history of the type in England, the occasion for its introduction, and the causes and stages of its decline.

The second and third of these parts, the research for which has already in large measure been done, I have reserved for future publication. The present thesis is a partial introduction to this more comprehensive work, and deals closely with the most famous genre of the period, commonly called the heroic drama. Broadly speaking, the adjective "heroic" in its connection with English dramatic literature would be applicable to many plays of the early seventeenth century (with particular appropriateness to those in which there was an infusion of Spanish ideals of love and honor), and also to some eighteenth century tragedies in which the dramatic modes of the immediately preceding ages were faintly reflected. But in the strict sense, the term "heroic play" refers to a short-lived kind of drama which arose in the reign of Charles II, and disappeared at the dawn of the following century. The plays were called heroic partly because they were written in heroic verse. The heroic manner, however, without changing its own nature, irregularly broke through the couplet with which it was primarily identified, and toward which its relation was always arbitrary and artificial. It was thus much more than a matter of form. It was concerned with plot; it dictated characterization; and it permeated with a certain sentiment the dramatic types with which it came in contact. The present essay considers the plot, characterization, and sentiment of the rhymed plays of the Restoration under this larger interpretation; consequently the discussion, although limited to rhymed plays, extends substantially to the whole manner of Restoration tragedy.

The main study is nevertheless strictly limited, in intent, to an examination of the type in its extant examples in literary texts. It does not enter upon the question of sources, nor of stage presentation, nor of historical development. It aims simply to describe the matter of the heroic play, much of which is rare and generally inaccessible, if not forgotten; and to furnish with this description a careful analysis of its structure and psychology such as will establish common traits. It is designed for special students of Restoration drama, and differs from preceding accounts in that it treats practically the entire body of the rhymed plays of the Restoration as a whole, and not as the work of individual writers. The rhymed plays of the leading dramatists of the period have been discussed in all biographies and critical estimates of their respective authors. But as Dryden was not only the central figure of the time, but also the foremost writer of heroic plays, the great mass of comment on the kind, with copious illustrations from his dramas, is to be sought under a Dryden bibliography.

Johnson, Scott, Saintsbury, Gosse, Garnett, and Beljame are some of the chief authorities, not to mention numerous others of reputation, who have considered the subject incidentally and in part. Holzhausen alone, I believe, has written at length on Dryden's heroic plays. Genest mentions a greater number of heroic plays in more detail than any other writer, and Ward's standard history notes the best of them and contains a valuable summary on the species. To these authorities and to other commentators on Restoration literature I desire to express an indebtedness the extent of which the Index and footnotes indicate.

The standard editions of D'Avenant, Etheridge, Dryden, Crowne, Otway, and Lee have been used, and the first editions of the other dramatists (in some instances the only editions), of which there is a large number in the Columbia University Library. I am glad to take this opportunity to thank the Librarian and his Assistants for their unfailing courtesy, which facilitated and made pleasanter my labors. My friend and associate, Dr. Horatio Sheafe Krans, rendered me assistance by suggestions and proof corrections which were of great value and for which I thank him. But to Professor George Edward Woodberry my obligation has been constant, and my appreciation of his kindly services is greater than can be expressed here. For a period of many years he has been my friend and master. He suggested this study to me, and throughout its evolution, in matters of general design and of minute detail, his constant interest and advice have been of the greatest aid.

L. N. C.

Columbia University, August 15, 1903.

CONTENTS

APPENDIX B

APPENDIX C

APPENDIX D

THE ENGLISH HEROIC PLAY

THE ENGLISH HEROIC PLAY

CHAPTER I

THE DEFINITION

THE heroic play employs as its characteristic verse form the pentameter rhyming in couplets or triplets or alternately, and uses besides various lyrical metres, and also blank verse and prose. Triplets are scattered throughout the entire body with noticeable frequency, and without obvious reason except, possibly, for the sake of varying the monotony. Their presence on the printed page is usually marked by brackets, and in some plays — perhaps rather in some writers — their large number leaves the impression of a mannerism of style. Their use does not serve so much to vary the form as to intensify the rhyme. There are, however, rare instances of a fine appropriateness to the subject and a consequent heightening of poetic effect due to their presence, as notably in the charm scene of the second act of "Henry III."[1] A line of less than ten syllables is sometimes employed. Thus the favorite metre of the "Siege of Rhodes"[2] is a line half the length of the pentameter. This form is repeated infrequently in later plays, although the use of it and of other broken lines is one of the evidences of Dryden's maturing mastery of versification; in other writers it is hard to decide whether the form is introduced through carelessness or for intentional variety. The numerous songs interspersed throughout the text are written in the conventional seventeenth century metres. Prose was considered as peculiarly the language of comedy, and in plays of that sort the evenness of the tone is maintained by that form. The more serious or lofty scenes of comedy, when not in prose, are occasionally in rhyme, generally in blank verse.

The presence of the heroic couplet has always been deemed, from Dryden's notes to the most

[1] "Henry the Third of France stabb'd by a Fryer with the Fall of the Guise." By Thomas Shipman. 1678.

[2] "Siege of Rhodes." By Sir William D'Avenant. 1656. This was the first edition, but subsequently the play was changed and enlarged. See Appendix C.

recent authorities, the *sine qua non* of an heroic play. "Heroic or rhyming plays" they have been called repeatedly, and without arousing discussion. Dryden, Rymer,[1] and Genest[2] have framed or indorsed this conception and have made it perfectly clear. It is legitimate to maintain this definition, and a sense of precision and a desire for a certain unity prompt its adoption here; else the term "heroic play"

[1] If other sources of information were wanting as to a definition of this species at the time of its popularity, Rymer's words would be of great weight, because he speaks with the authority of a schoolmaster, with a pedant's fondness for precise statement. In the Advertisement to "Edgar; or the English Monarch," 1678, he says, "This I call an Heroick Tragedy, having in it chiefly sought occasions to extoll the *English* Monarchy; and having writ it in that Verse which with *Cowley*, *Denham*, and *Waller*, I take to be most proper for Epic Poetry." A heroic play, therefore, must be in rhyme, and the use of the words "extoll" and "epic" mean that it shall be in the exalted manner proper to heroes of romance. Incidentally, Dryden's usual phrase is "Heroic Play"; Langbaine's, "a Tragedy writ in Heroic Verse"; whereas "Heroic Tragedy" which has become equally with "Heroic Play" the common designation for this kind of drama, is on the title-page of only one composition of its class, and that is "Edgar."

[2] "At this time any Tragedy written in rhyme was considered as a heroick play." — JOHN GENEST, "English Stage. Some Account of the English Stage from the Restoration," etc., 1832, i. 223.

becomes a matter of sentiment entirely divorced from all form, its nature changed through dissipation, and its boundaries extended to a time as yet undetermined. Ward's phrase, "heroic tragedy in rhyme," which would have been thought a tautology in the seventeenth century, indicates the growing sense of the possibility of a discussion of the heroic element apart from rhyme; and in his criticism of "Heroick Love,"[1] he breaks away from the established tradition. "This play, though written in blank verse, may so far be regarded as a signal example of 'heroic' tragedy, that its whole action tends to turn on the one passion of love — the 'universal passion,' truly, of the tragic dramatists of this period."[2] Unfortunately a determination of the nature of heroic love — considerable contribution as it would be — would not exhaust heroic sentiment.

Yet it must be admitted, that if only such plays as are wholly in rhyme are to be regarded as heroic the number is too small to account

[1] "Heroick Love, or the Cruel Separation." By George Granville, Lord Lansdowne. 1698.

[2] A. W. Ward, "A History of English Dramatic Literature to the Death of Queen Anne." A new and revised edition (1899), iii. 424.

for the furore they made in their own generation. The term must have been applied to plays partly so written; but such an admission weakens the force of the definition. Unless it can be shown that in a play containing prose, blank verse, and rhyme, the last named has a function distinct from the others, then the limitation of rhyme in the definition must be regarded as arbitrary. But, as a matter of fact, the function of rhyme is not evident; or, to be bolder, there are numerous passages in several plays that make the conclusion unavoidable that the use of any one of the three forms just mentioned rather than any other, particularly the choice between blank verse and rhyme, is accidental and capricious. The candid author of "Great Favourite" gives the true state of the case: "I will not therefore pretend to say, why I writ this Play, some Scenes in blank Verse, others in Rhyme, since I have no better a reason to give then Chance, which waited upon my present Fancy; and I expect no better a reason from any ingenious person, then his Fancy for which he best relishes."[1]

[1] "Great Favourite, or the Duke of Lerma." By Sir Robert Howard. 1668. To the Reader.

An inspection of the play itself, which is mainly written in blank verse, seems to justify this remark, especially in the fourth and last acts. A strange instance of the mingling of forms is found in the "Destruction of Troy."[1] This play, which also is mainly in blank verse, breaks into couplets so irregularly that it seems as if the author were uncertain, when he began a line, whether it would end in a rhyme or not. The "Sacrifice"[2] is another example of the indiscriminate use of the three forms. The search for system is nowhere more interesting and nowhere more futile than in "Marcelia."[3] Dryden's versification has been pretty thoroughly investigated, especially the growth of his technical skill. The mixed passages of blank verse and rhyme in which his irresolution and uncertainty are displayed further illustrate the absence of any fixed usage in the employment of rhyme as a necessary element in the heroic play.

[1] "Destruction of Troy." By John Bankes. 1679.

[2] "Sacrifice." By Sir Francis Fane. 1686.

[3] "Marcelia, or the Treacherous Friend." By Mrs. F. Boothby. 1670.

CHAPTER II

PLOT

THE heroic element in Restoration drama is in itself tolerably distinct and easily ascertainable wherever found, at least in its early phases. Its introduction into English dramatic literature was an innovation, and from the first so dominated certain theatrical productions of many sorts that, whatever their genre, they became, in fact, heroic plays. Yet this element was not from the first, nor ever after, peculiar to any single dramatic form, but inserted itself into them all in varying degrees and with varying success. It worked its way into the opera, comedy, tragicomedy, history, and tragedy of the day, without altering their respective moulds, no matter how it affected their tone.

The origin of the English heroic play and of the English opera was simultaneous. The "Siege of Rhodes" has been called, and with reason, the first heroic play; and with reason, also, it has been called the first English opera. That is not to say that it is completely one or the other; but toward both it stands, if as nothing more, "in an indistinct relation of parentage."[1] The author styled it an opera, and thus introduced a new word into the language.[2] In so far as it contained singing or chanting, as part of the action, not extraneous to it, the "Siege of Rhodes" was legitimately operatic. In paying unprecedented attention to scenery and pageantry (crude as it was in these respects in comparison with its successors), it began in England the tradition, which had long been in force on the Continent, that the spectacle was a necessary operatic feature, distinguishing the opera hardly less than vocal music from drama proper. So Langbaine says of

[1] Ward, iii. 328, where the phrase is applied only to opera.

[2] His reason for using the word seems to have been almost entirely commercial, without much consideration of fitness. It was necessary to hoodwink the Puritan police authorities in order to give the production. Modern parallels are common. "Long after he had dismissed the music and produced regular tragedies he adhered to the word opera, the use of which had enabled him to steer his bark in 'ticklish times.'" — JOSEPH KNIGHT, Historical Preface to John Downes, "Roscius Anglicanus," etc., 1886.

"Circe"[1]: "The Scenes and Machines may give it a Title to that Species of Dramatick Poetry, call'd an Opera."[2] It is almost needless to state that this tradition, in spite of impecuniousness and consequent bareness of operatic productions from time to time, has been continuous.

The "Siege of Rhodes" is heroic in that it is written in rhyme, partly in heroic couplets; it has a war background; it is a story of love, with its usual ingredient of jealousy and of honor;[3] and it contains argumentation in verse.[4] That the opera and the heroic play should have first manifested themselves in England precisely at the same time in the same production is curious, and appears almost accidental; but this fact linked their names

[1] "Circe." By Charles D'Avenant, LL.D. 1677.

[2] Gerard Langbaine, "An Account of the English Dramatick Poets," etc., 1691, p. 116. "The *machines* were as essential to opera as the music and poetry, and the artists of the scenery and dresses were at least the equal of the poet and musical composer." Dryden's Essays, edited by W. P. Ker, i. lxv–lxvi. 1890.

[3] "Well calculated to please when Love and Honour were the order of the day." Genest, i. 39.

[4] Scene between Solyman and Ianthe in Act 3, Pt. 2, and between Solyman and Roxolana, Act 4.

together far more closely than events justified, for it was not the operatic features that made the piece heroic, or vice versa. There are many heroic plays in which such features are wanting; and so the statement that the kind "always retained some tinge" of the opera,[1] is not strictly warrantable. They were essentially different in kind, and the former could be independent of the other. Their relationship, however, was intimate.

It is to be remembered, first, that in this period music took its permanent abode in the theatre. Henceforth, the playhouse and the music-house were to be one and the same. The English people had always been rich in folk-songs; but these, like the ballads, which were their nearest literary counterpart, were unrecognized among the learned, and homeless, except in the common heart. Music fared better than its sister art under the Commonwealth, principally perhaps because of Cromwell's liking for it; but on the Restoration it seems to have been recognized for the first time as a necessary adjunct to the theatre. "A regular

[1] George Saintsbury, "Life of Dryden," English Men of Letters Series, p. 18.

band of musicians was placed in the orchestra, who, between the acts, performed pieces of music composed for that purpose and called act-tunes ; and also accompanied the vocal music sung on the stage, and played the music of the dances. Music thus became attached to the theatres, which from this time became the principal nurseries of musicians, both composers and performers. The most favorite music was that which was heard in the dramatic pieces of the day ; and to sing and play the songs, dances, and act-tunes of the theatre became a general amusement in fashionable society."[1] Doubtless this attention to the art of music in public places encouraged its practice among the people. Pepys's passion for it is typical. The recent revival of interest and consequent investigation of music of this period have revealed a knowledge and mastery, among amateurs, hitherto unsuspected, while there were professional performers of world fame, native musicians of the first rank, and Purcell, probably England's most distinguished and most remarkable composer. There is good evidence that skill in technique steadily improved from the cor-

[1] George Hogarth, "Memoirs of the Opera," 1851, i. 78–79.

onation to the end of the century.[1] This increasing popularity and cultivation of the art were shown in all sorts of theatrical performances. The opera and the heroic play arose simultaneously with this interest, — the first essentially musical, and the other capable of assimilating operatic features without losing its character. They were both produced on the same stage, by the same people,[2] for the same audience; thus their intimate connection on the external side is manifest. The resemblance, however, is more than external, for in the second place both forms are written in rhyme;[3] but whereas the former in its purity is entirely in heroic couplets, the latter is in a variety of metres; and whereas the former was an importation avowedly introduced into England to please the king, operas are in rhyme to enhance

[1] "All this while play-house music improved yearly, and is arrived to greater perfection than ever I knew it." — JAMES WRIGHT, "Historia Histrionica," 1699.

[2] Cf. Hogarth, i. 143 ff., for the names of some actors who were also singers. Among them were Harris, Mountfort, Mary Davis and Mrs. Bracegirdle.

[3] "The libretto of an *opera* is a peculiar kind of drama entirely in verse and set to music, and partly in prose to be spoken." — A. HENNEQUIN, "Art of Playwriting," 1890, p. 49.

the lyric effect and to facilitate the singer's execution. When an opera is mainly in pentameters, as Dr. Charles D'Avenant's "Circe," it indicates the influence of the heroic play upon the other form, as this kind of verse is in itself but ill suited to operatic uses.

The third likeness between the two is that the matter of both is love. But here again the difference in source makes more patent the difference in kind. Love in the heroic plays was an exotic that never existed anywhere, least of all in England, and was put into dramatic form to please and appease the same people that read the current romances ; while love was then and always the main subject of the opera, not primarily because it reflected a transitory fashion (although one is not easily distinguishable from the other as shown in Restoration art, so pervasive was the heroic quality), but rather because love is of all the passions the one for which music is the most natural voice.[1]

The union of the heroic and the operatic was a natural, and not, in the main, a contradictory alliance. As much cannot be said of the meeting, within the same play, of the heroic and the

[1] See Appendix A.

comic. The heroic characteristic of exalted sentiment is opposed to the spirit of comedy, most of all to the comedy spirit of the Restoration. And yet at the very outset of its career, it entered comedy, for the "Comical Revenge,"[1] 1664, was "the earliest regular play in which the use of rime was actually attempted, unless its isolated application by Dryden in two passages of 'Rival Ladies,' 1663,[2] be taken into account. Etheridge therefore was courageous enough to carry out in a regular comedy the innovations which D'Avenant had employed in an 'operatic' entertainment, and on behalf of which Dryden had argued."[3]

The comedy of this era was the most rigidly defined of all the current dramatic types. It began early in the sixties, and although its brightest lights did not shine for upwards of thirty or forty years, it early reached a mature and self-contented state. Considering the vast body of plays it embraces, the term, "comedy of manners," is a peculiarly adequate and satis-

[1] "Comical Revenge, or, Love in a Tub." By Sir George Etheridge. 1664.

[2] "Rival Ladies." By John Dryden. 1664.

[3] Ward, iii. 444.

factory designation. Nothing could be more anti-heroic either in intent or practice. To satirize the foibles of the age was its object; but neither with satire nor with foibles, nor with any particular age was the heroic sentiment of Restoration drama concerned. And as for diction, the "comic dramatists, with the exception of a very few experiments, confine themselves to the use of prose."[1] Well defined and, in general, strictly adhered to as the separation between comedy and tragedy was, the gulf between the comic and the heroic manner was even wider; for whereas there is at least one contemporary comedy in blank verse,[2] one in rhyme is yet to be discovered;[3] the presence of rhyme, moreover, was accompanied with sufficient change in the treatment of the subject-matter, if not in the subject-matter itself, to render the title "comedy," as it was then used, inappropriate.

[1] Ward, iii. 498.

[2] "Married Beau, or the Curious Impertinent." By John Crowne. 1694.

[3] Certain French comedies were translated into English rhyme; and although the greater part of serious scenes in Restoration comedy, not in prose, are written in blank verse, some are in rhyme.

The heroic element, when introduced into comedy, had a more revolutionary effect than it had upon any other type. To the opera, it was not, on the whole, antagonistic, and tragedy was its home. It transformed comedies into something different, usually called tragicomedies; but whereas comedy was a firmly established form, tragicomedy has always been a makeshift term, brought into more or less use [1] according to the narrow or liberal interpretation of the two types which it has sought to blend. It has been described as a species "resembling the regular Tragedy in its outward form, but containing some comic characters, and always having a happy termination;" [2] and also referred to as that "mixed species which came to be called (but by no consistent usage) *tragicomedy*." [3] Genest says, that "Ormasdes" [4] was "called a T. C. as no person is killed, but there are no comic scenes, — the whole is serious." [5] There are three so-called tragicomedies

[1] There were more than fifty plays of this class from 1656 to 1703.

[2] J. W. Donaldson, "Theatre of the Greeks," 1860 (seventh ed.), p. 75.

[3] Ward, i. 210.

[4] "Ormasdes." By Sir William Killigrew. 1665.

[5] Genest, x. 139.

with an heroic element: "Amazon Queen,"[1] "Rival Ladies," and "Marcelia." The first is entirely, the others partly, in rhyme. "Marcelia" and "Rival Ladies" contain distinct comic characters and incidents, but no more so than "Altemira"[2] and "Fatal Jealousie,"[3] which were called tragedies. The "Comical Revenge," with no designation on the title-page, was considered a comedy by contemporaries—Evelyn, Downes, Langbaine; but Ward[4] takes pains to use the prefix. Dryden himself styled the "Rival Ladies" a tragicomedy; but he called "Marriage-a-la-Mode"[5] a comedy, which Langbaine thus takes exception to; "This play, though stil'd in the Title-page as Comedy, is rather a Tragicomedy, and consists of two different actions; the one serious, the other Comick."[6] He is followed by Genest.

The form of drama called histories, so numerous in the Elizabethan era, were exceedingly

[1] "Amazon Queen, or the Amours of Thalestris to Alexander the Great." By Jo. Weston. 1667.

[2] "Altemira." By Roger Boyle, Earl of Orrery. 1702.

[3] "Fatal Jealousie." By Henry Neville Payne (?). 1674.

[4] Ward, iii. 498 n.

[5] "Marriage-a-la-Mode." By John Dryden. 1673.

[6] Langbaine, p. 166.

and significantly rare in the last half of the century. There seem to have been no more than four so styled, of which two are heroic plays. There is nothing in either of them that would prevent their being placed under the head of tragedy, as tragedy was then interpreted. This applies the more strictly to "Charles VIII,"[1] whereas the claim of "Henry V"[2] for consideration under any recognized dramatic type would be easy to disprove. It has none of the characteristics of Restoration comedy; its tone is more serene and unperturbed throughout than that of any other tragedy, if such it be, while the much-abused historical novel, in its most untruthful phases, is a slave to fact in comparison with this play in indebtedness to historical truth. It is doubtless because of the mere frequent mention of historic figures and events, regardless of most amazing twistings of fact and additions of fiction, that these plays were called histories.

The authors did not always please to designate the kind of composition on the title-page

[1] "The History of Charles the Eighth of France, or the Invasion of Naples by the French." By John Crowne. 1672.

[2] "The History of Henry the Fifth." By Roger Boyle, Earl of Orrery. 1669.

of the play or elsewhere. This omission seldom causes confusion, because the term "tragedy" was applied liberally, not to say inconsistently on the whole, or rashly. Sometimes the writer uses the term where the critic seems surprised at its use. Thus Genest remarks of the "Libertine"[1]: "As there is Superabundance of murder in this play it is called a Tragedy, but the dialogue is in great measure Comic." The obvious construction of Langbaine's comment on the application of the term to the "Black Prince"[2] is that he considered such use uncommon. "Tho this Play in the Title-page be call'd a Tragedy, yet it ends successfully: and therefore I presume was rather stiled so by the Author from the Quality and Grandeur of the Persons in the Drama, than from any unfortunate Catastrophe." There were indeed two forms of tragedy, the main difference depending on the fortunate or unfortunate catastrophe. "The Tragedy ends Prosperously," says Rymer in the Advertisement to his own play, "Edgar": "A sort of Tragedy that rarely succeeds; man being apter to pity the

[1] "Libertine." By Thomas Shadwell. 1676.

[2] "Black Prince." By Roger Boyle, Earl of Orrery. 1669.

Distressed, then to rejoyce with the Prosperous. Yet this sort seems principally to have pleased Euripides ; and is necessary here."

Investigation shows, however, that tragedies with happy ending were neither uncommon or unsuccessful. Tragedy was the natural abiding-place of the heroic element. With comedy it was unsympathetic; its relation to opera was appreciably accidental; but in tragedy it was at home. So closely and yet rightly are they associated that the terms "heroic play" and "heroic tragedy" have always been used without discrimination. The "Quality and Grandeur" of heroic characters was peculiar to no other form than tragedy. In fact all phases of heroic diction and sentiment might be readily construed as appropriate to tragedy. The presence of the heroic element did not alter or disturb the main drift of the tragic form which includes an unhappy termination. Up to that time unhappy catastrophe had been so much the rule as to be commonly considered essential ; but in the heroic element, as such, there was nought to necessitate such an ending. It might, perhaps, be insisted upon that an unsuccessful termination is out of accord with the hero's character, where frequently the success of marvellous actions justified the usual accompanying boast. There were nearly as many heroic tragedies of prosperous conclusion as of the other sort; and this large number might reasonably be attributed to the presence and influence of the heroic element.

The "Conquest of Granada"[1] is the most illustrious of this kind. The fall of the city is not the main matter, but rather the deeds of Almanzor; his success is literally the most prolonged of any in English dramatic literature, by five acts, as the play is in ten. Generally, of course, it is easy enough to distinguish between a happy and an unfortunate conclusion; but occasionally there is chance for difference. In the "Conquest of China"[2] there is a "superabundance of murder," yet the murdered are all villains and the righteous survive. Where the principal character is a villain, in the end he is usually punished; but in such cases much depends on the importance of other char-

[1] "Almanzor and Almahide, or the Conquest of Granada by the Spaniards." By John Dryden. 1672.

[2] "Conquest of China by the Tartars." By Elkanah Settle. 1676.

acters, and to what extent he is preëminent over them. Richard III's fate is not so fraught with tragic consequences in the "English Princess"[1] as in the Shakespearean play. In the latter, the leading interests are his character and his relation to England, so his death is more deeply and widely significant than in the former where the sole theme is love; Richard is the unsuccessful suitor for the princess's hand, and his fortunate rival is Richmond; his death removes the obstacle to their marriage. Perhaps the termination of the "Rival Kings"[2] is on the whole fortunate, and still one of the surviving heroes exclaims:

> "We purchase pleasure, almost with despair."

In "Edgar," likewise, although the principal lovers survive, their joy is hardly conceivable, so dearly is it bought. It should be observed that the chief traits of the modern melodrama, which are exaggerated sentiment and a happy termination after dire misgivings, were first popularized in the heroic tragedy.

[1] "English Princess or the Death of Richard III." [By John Caryl] 1667.

[2] "Rival Kings, or the Loves of Oroondates and Statira." By John Bankes. 1677.

It is mainly as tragedy, therefore, that the heroic play is to be regarded. The pattern came from France directly with the many borrowings of the Merry Monarch. There was then no judgment exercised as to the suitability of the imported articles for native use, but everything French was brought into England wholesale, at random, and without reason. The native character of the importations was so ill comprehended that the foreign taste in drama was no less ridiculous than in clothes, and quite as extensive and obvious. There is fashion in plays as well as clothes, Dryden says; and just as the summer Parisian styles did not reach London, in those days of slow communication, until winter, and yet as soon as they came were donned straightway regardless of the season, as one of the comedies states, just so the French form of tragedy was welcomed in England, with rhyme, but without reason, and though it soon drifted away in spirit from its origin, it remained to the end foreign, exotic, un-English.

The imitation of the French manner in the heroic play was manifested most considerably in the construction of the plot. It is not a question of where the stories came from in the first place, but how they were handled after their introduction into England. As laziness occasioned, according to Shadwell[1] the borrowings from France, so absence of originality or of any deviation from what was considered the French manner is the most noticeable characteristic of the external form of heroic plays.

The real unlikeness, however, between the genuine French manner and what was considered as such in England should be borne in mind. It is not surprising that French sentiment and spirit in contact with the English should undergo transformation. Imitation, nevertheless, is most patent in the technical, almost manual labor of playwriting. But even here allowance is to be made for certain discrepancies between the original and the imitation, arising fundamentally from the difference in the genius of the two peoples.

The French manner, as it was interpreted, was formulated into a code of precise rules so minute, and withal so comprehensive, that any sign of originality on the part of the aspirant

[1] Preface to the "Miser."

for dramatic honors would seem superfluous and out of place. These rules were readily conned and applied, else there would not have been so many plays put on the boards. That Dryden produced six in one year, and Settle wrote "Cambyses"[1] when he was eighteen, shows the easiness of the feat.

The first and foremost of those rules was regard of the three unities. With a very few exceptions[2] all heroic plays observe them, or more correctly, there is no tangible evidence to the contrary. Complete silence on the subject, either within the text or elsewhere, regarding the time supposed to have passed between the first and last act, makes judgment difficult. Still, it may be assumed, when the unities of action and place are observed and nothing is said about the time, that the last, also, is respected. It is the only one that seems to cause the authors embarrassment.[3] Generally, direct mention of it is avoided; sometimes a queen

[1] "Cambyses, King of Persia." By Elkanah Settle. 1671.

[2] "Henry III." "The Scene *Blois* remov'd at th' Fourth Act to the Camp at *St. Clou* before Paris." In "Marcelia" the scene is at Lyons and Marseilles.

[3] As in "Henry III," Act 2.

asking the king for permission to occupy the throne for three days,[1] and the not uncommon crowding of more than one battle into the time given, perhaps justify the conclusion that the time-limit may have been extended beyond twenty-four hours; but, even so, the strict observance of the other unities suggests the probability of a liberal interpretation here rather than a wilful breach.[2] Observance of unity of action was responsible for the general sameness of tone, which implied the restriction if not the exclusion of the comic; and the unity of action once in force, the others follow naturally.[3] The following quotation from Langbaine shows the current deference toward the unities and also the difficulty of getting the mass of the people to appreciate correctness:

"I must say this for our countrymen. That notwithstanding our modern authors have borrow'd much from the French, and other

[1] "Siege of Memphis, or the Ambitious Queen." By Thomas Durfey. 1676.

[2] Now and then attention is called to the strict observance of them all, as in the Prologue to the "Maiden Queen" and the statement prefixed to "Edgar": "The time of the Representation from Twelve at Noon to Ten at Night."

[3] Thomas Rymer, "The Tragedies of the Last Age," etc., 1678, p. 24.

nations, yet have we several Pieces, if I may so say, of our own manufacture which equal at least, any of our neighbours productions. This is a truth so generally known, that I need not bring instances to prove, that in the humour of our comedies, and in the characters of our tragedies, we do not yield to any other nation. 'Tis true that the unities of Time, Place and Action, which are generally allowed to be the Beauties of a Play, and which the French are so careful to observe, add all Lusture to their Plays; nevertheless several of our poets have given proof, that did our Nation more regard them, they could practice them with equal success: But as a correct play is not so much understood, or at least regarded by the generality of Spectators, and that few of our Poets now-a-days write so much for Honour as Profit, they are therefore content to please at an easier rate."[1]

Jacob's criticism of Granville's "Heroick Love" notes his observance of the "strictest rules of the ancient drama."

"A Tragedy acted at the Theatre Royal with great applause. This play is one of the best of our modern Tragedies. His Lordship has observed the strictest rules of the ancient Drama; the Action is single, the Place not varied, nor the Time extended beyond Aristotle's Bounds; the whole being transacted in the

[1] Gerard Langbaine, "Momus Triumphans," etc., 1688. Preface.

same Camp, and requiring no more hours than are barely necessary for the Representation. He has, perhaps, too industriously avoided that crowd of Incident which the English Stage seems to demand. His Lordship has likewise broke through that long established Custom of Stabbing and Murdering upon the Stage, not one actor being represented as dying in the sight of the Audience, which gave occasion to some Criticks to except against it as Tragedy; as if the fatal and unavoidable necessity of an Eternal separation between two faithful Lovers was not a catastrophe sufficiently moving; or that cruel unnatural and bloody Spectacle were the Essentials of the Tragedy. His Lordship, in this play, seems by his style to have made it his chief study to deliver the Tragick Vein from all fustian and affected Expressions and to preserve the Dignity of the Buskin from sinking too low or rising too high."[1]

There are other laws that a tragic poet should observe, the greater part of which were expressed by Rymer. Indeed, the "Tragedies of the Last Age" may be considered as a standard text-book on the subject. Here are some of its dicta:

"The Fable is the soul of a Tragedy." "The Argument, Plot or Fable for a Tragedy

[1] [Giles Jacob], "The Poetical Register," etc., 1723. i. 123.

ought to be taken from History."[1] The English err in putting too wicked persons on the stage.[2]

These are but remnants of a long dramatic tradition, and do not pretend to individual authorship. It is questionable, however, if Aristotle would admit that the idea that in poetry all kings are necessarily heroes was based on the "theory and practice of the ancients." "Though it is not necessary that all *heroes* should be Kings, yet undoubtedly all crown'd heads, by *Poetical right*, are *Heroes*. This Character is a flower, a prerogative, so certain, so indispensably annexed to the *Crown* as by no Poet, or *Parliament* of poets, ever to be invaded."[3]

There are, it seems, most binding laws of duel in tragedy.

"If I mistake not, in Poetry no woman is to kill a man, except her quality gives her

[1] Rymer, Contents.

[2] Rymer, *passim.* Cf. Jacob's (i. 210) criticism of Ravencroft's "Italian Husband": "This poet seems to be under the same Mistake with some other of our modern writers, who are fond of barbarous and bloody Stories, and think no Tragedy can be good without some Villain in it."

[3] Rymer, p. 61.

the advantage above him; nor is a Servant to kill the Master, nor a Private Man, much less a Subject to kill a King, nor on the contrary. Poetical decency will not suffer death to be dealt to each other, by such persons whom the Laws of Duel allow not to enter the lists together. There may be circumstances that alter the case, as where there is sufficient ground of partiality in an *Audience*, either upon the account of *religion* (as *Rinaldo*, or *Riccardo*, in *Tasso*, might kill *Soliman*, or any other *Turkish* King or great *Sultan*) or else in favour of our *country*, for then a private *English heroe* might overcome a King of some Rival Nation."[1]

Rymer is the laughing-stock of the modern critical world — probably the worst critic that ever lived, Macaulay bluntly remarks. But all that he said is of special and of great significance historically, because it was supposed both by himself and intelligent contemporaries to rest upon a learned and philosophic foundation. Dryden, Pope, and Dr. Johnson admired

[1] Rymer, pp. 117-118. T. N. Talfourd's comment on this passage is worth quoting:

"How pleasant a master of ceremonies is he in the regions of fiction, regulating the niceties of murder like the decorums of a dance, with an amiable preference for his own religion and country!" *Retrospective Review*, i. 1 (1820), "Rymer on Tragedy."

and respected him. Besides giving utterance to principles current in his day, he embodied them in one of the most correct heroic plays ever written, and not only correct but typical of many features of plot construction then in vogue. That it was almost worthless as dramatic literature in nowise distinguished it from many others of its kind. Addison called attention to its failure as if that were unique, for it never saw the light of day, it was never put on the stage, it died as a living play before it was born. But neither is that enough to distinguish it from the others. That it died young whereas the others survived it a few years, and then expired, as they all did without exception, does not make it different in kind from them. It was printed in at least three different years; as much cannot be said of some of its apparently more successful rivals. And, after all, Rymer and Addison — not to make the generalization include others — were alike distinguished critics who wrote plays of perfect correctness and lifelessness.

On the whole there was little protest against the form of the heroic play, for it was a phase of the recognized tragic form of all Europe.

Yet one author claims that his piece is not "dress'd by Rules of Art,"[1] and another makes a plea for freedom of taste even in the determination of types:

"I must ingeniously confess, that the manner of Plays which now are in most esteem, is beyond my pow'r to perform; nor do I condemn in the least anything of what Nature soever that pleases; since nothing cou'd appear to me a ruder folly, than to censure the satisfaction of others; I rather blame the unnecessary understanding of some that are not Mathematical, and with such eagerness, pursuing their own seeming reasons, that at last we are to apprehend such Argumentative Poets will grow as strict as *Sancho Pancos* Doctor was to our very Appetites; for in the difference of *Tragedy* and *Comedy*, and of *Fars* it self, there can be no determination but by the Taste; nor in the manner of their Composure; and whoever wou'd endeavour to like or dislike by the Rules of others, he will be as unsuccessful, as if he should try to be persuaded into a power of believing; not what he must, but what others direct him to believe."[2]

To the statement that "in the difference of tragedy, comedy, and farce itself, there can be no determination but by the taste," Dryden

[1] "Fatal Jealousie." Epilogue.

[2] "Great Favourite." To the Reader.

answered: "I will not quarrel with the obscurity of his phrase, though I justly might; but beg his pardon if I do not rightly understand him. If he means that there is no essential difference between comedy, tragedy, and farce, but what is made only by the people's taste, which distinguishes one of them from the other, that is so manifest an error, that I need not lose time to contradict it. Were there neither judge, taste, nor opinion in the world, yet they would differ in their natures."[1]

Howard has been censured for both the tone and the content of his preface, yet it must have been the expression of more than a purely personal opinion, at a time when regularity was the school cry of the day.

The rank extravagance of language and of character that predominates in so many heroic plays does not so frequently belong to the plot. The regularity of the plot checks such a tendency. There are some plays in which much takes place, and the course of events seems unrestrained. They are obviously the more conspicuous, perhaps the more interesting. Extravagance in both characterization and plot

[1] Dryden, "A Defence of an Essay of Dramatic Poesy."

construction makes them more strikingly heroic than many others in which the plot is regular and stands out in marked contrast to the extravagance of diction and of character. There are yet others wherein all the elements are subdued, and where there is little rant or fustian, which are, none the less broadly characteristic of the heroic kind. Such is "Aureng-Zebe"[1]; and because it is nearer the Racine manner, calmer, more correct, with simpler plot, and characters truer to nature, the supernatural machinery omitted, and the dialogue not so extravagant, Holzhausen pronounces it not typical.[2]

Such another is "Love's Triumph."[3] No play more distinctly shows French influence in method of construction. There is much dialogue of a sort that does not advance the action; the situation is revealed in the first act, and there is no perceptible progress or change until the last, when one of the possible alternatives

[1] "Aureng-Zebe, or the Great Mogul." By John Dryden. 1676.

[2] Paul Holzhausen, "Dryden's Heroisches Drama," "Englische Studien," xiii. 443.

[3] "Love's Triumph, or the Royal Union." By Edward Cooke. 1678.

takes place. In "Caligula" the mildness of the plot is entirely unlike the extravagance of the character and sentiment. The time is confined to the last hour of the emperor's life, and there are long scenes devoid of action. In some plays the stage is crowded with incidents and characters, in others it is bare; some plots are simple, others complex.

Love and honor were theoretically the subjects of heroic plays, and so in one form or another the relation between them may be supposed to have been intended as the leading dramatic motive. The shape it assumed varied. In all but one of Orrery's heroic plays, friendship is a form of honor, and they are entirely concerned with the conflict between love and friendship, the friends being rivals in love.

A second form concerns four people, — a male and female villain, and a hero and his mistress. The male villain loves the mistress and the female villain the hero, so their alliance is founded on selfish interest. The pair of villains do all in their power to separate the lovers, but each villain is determined to defend the beloved object from harm, so they work at cross-purposes, and meanwhile the lovers are safe. In the end both villains are killed by opportune interference from outside.

A third manifestation of the same idea is where the female villain becomes infatuated with the hero, who is of course already a lover. She offers him the choice of reciprocating her passion or death. She meets her fate, likewise, through external interference that also saves him from the embarrassment of a decision; or she may be so successful as to bring about the death of his love, and possibly that of himself, before her own.

There are a few instances where the conflict, as to which of the rivals will win the lady, is purely physical. Sometimes the subject itself is unimportant. "Caligula,"[1] for example, is mainly an attempted character study, with little plot.

Such are some of the main themes, the raw material for a drama. But the essence of a play is in struggle, and it is here frequently lacking, the issue is evaded. "Henry V" has to do with love and honor, and in the case of one of the characters there is what passes for a conflict between them; but, such as it is, it is

[1] "Caligula." By John Crowne. 1698.

personal, individual, not influencing the play as a whole. The political and love elements, respectively, are not at all connected as contending for the fate of any character. Henry is warrior and lover, but he does not have to sacrifice one in order to be the other. As warrior, he has no obstacles to confront; as lover, but one (his friend's passion for the same lady) which he easily surmounts. There is no dramatic struggle because there is nothing to struggle against. The king says he will forego his crown before his love, but there is not the slightest possibility of such a contingency arising. With Tudor, the conflict, whether or not he shall be true to his friend and liege rather than to his love, is not real. The choice is not in his hands. He has been rejected before the question arises, and is again; so the issue is actually not whether he will be true to love or friendship, as evidently his author and himself desire it construed, but rather how manfully he will bear up under adversity in love. The real struggle has been done away with by the princess's preference for the king. Such is also the case in "Tryphon"[1] with Seleucus, an unsuc-

[1] "Tryphon." By Roger Boyle, Earl of Orrery. 1669.

cessful suitor who decides to force the object of his affection to marry him ; but there is no instance of a girl deciding in the first act not to marry a man ever after changing her mind, or being made to do so.

Constancy between the principal lovers of a play is practically invariable, and although the dramatic motive springs from the attempt of a jealous third person to win away the love of one of them, the initial and paramount error of all such persons arises from their belief, taken for granted, that the fear of death will induce lovers to part, and win them toward other loves; nor would the doing away of one of the lovers in any wise make the coast easy and clear for his hated rival; as for the threat of death, there is no more oft-reiterated note in the heroic kind than indifference toward or even desire for death. The lovers are given the choice of dying together or living apart; they decide on the former; but it is a matter of words; they are not put to the test.

On the issue of probability there was difference of opinion. For its sake, Rymer advocated adherence to history :

"We generally observe, when one tells of an adventure, or but a jest, he will choose to father it on some one that is known thereby to get attention, and gain more credit to what he relates. Besides, many things are probable of Antoninus, or of Alexander, and particular men, because they are true, which cannot be generally probable: and he that will be feigning persons should confine his fancy to general probability." [1]

This is one way, and there are some heroic plays that did not violate the dictum. On the other hand, Dryden [2] differentiated heroic plays from other tragedies in that they were not subject to the laws of probability. It is by this very disregard of necessary sequence that a large number of heroic plays differ from genuine dramas.[3]

There is only one of Dryden's heroic plays

[1] Rymer, p. 17.

[2] His own dramatic irresponsibility is shown by his deeming it necessary to print for distribution and circulation in the audience an explanation of one of his plays, the "Indian Emperor," where the play failed to explain itself.

[3] Orrery, when the long letter he inserted in the "Black Prince" was hissed, had it printed and copies handed to the spectators. The boldest disregard of a necessary dramatic sequence, however, is in the "Vestal Virgin," which has two last acts, one comic, the other tragic, either of which was substituted for the other at will.

where a single dramatic idea is carried out.[1] What is to be expected, therefore, of lesser men? Of what consequence in comparison with the radical fault of the lack of a single dramatic idea, and of total disregard of dramatic responsibility are all other defects of plot construction?[2] Vain is the search for inherent relation between plot and character. A study of the

[1] "Tyrannic Love." Cf. Holzhausen, E. S., xiii. 432.

[2] Such defects are naturally numerous, and some of them were first commented on by the authors themselves. Otway writes of his first play: "I found myself father of a dramatic birth which I called 'Alcibiades' (1675); but I might, without offence to any person in the play, as well have called it 'Nebuchadnezzar.'" (Preface to "Don Carlos.") Ward likens its plot to a nightmare.

The weakness of the plot of the "Maiden Queen" is suggested in the Preface to that play, and commented on by Ward. The same critic speaks of the absence of combination of external and intrinsic interest in "Don Carlos." The weakness of the plot of "Caligula" is noted by Maidment and Logan, and that of "Mustapha" by Dryden. Jacob calls attention to the plot absurdities in the "State of Innocence."

Notice further the sudden transformation from the usurping king to the kindly father-in-law in "Marriage-a-la-Mode," the unfortunate title of "Sophonisba, or Hannibal's Overthrow," inasmuch as Sophonisba had nothing to do with Hannibal's overthrow. In fact, Massinissa, as an ally of Scipio, was the chief factor in bringing about Hannibal's defeat; and Sophonisba's conquest over him took him from battle and thus increased Hannibal's chances of success.

plot in Restoration tragedy is a study of externals. The raw material was imported and manipulated by novices who had a text-book knowledge of the subject, without the slightest comprehension of the relation between external and internal form.

CHAPTER III

CHARACTER

One of the most obvious differences between the Elizabethan and Restoration drama—a phase of the movement toward greater external unity—is in the variety of characters. The strongest indication that the Restoration plays were to be more limited in character range than the earlier is that there were fewer characters to deal with. Narrow range does not necessarily follow as a result of the small number of characters in several plays of the same period, any more than a limited vocabulary necessarily implies a contracted mind. But words beget thoughts as truly as thoughts beget words. It is not by accident that Shakespeare's wealth of thought is expressed in the largest vocabulary ever used, and the bare fact that his *dramatis personæ* are great in number suggests, if it does not indirectly state, that the variety is proportionately considerable. In Orrery's "Henry V" there are nineteen names in the cast, in Shakespeare twenty-seven (omitting the chorus); in Caryl's "English Princess, or the Death of Richard III," there are seventeen; in the corresponding tragedy of Shakespeare, thirty-five; and in Sedley's "Antony and Cleopatra"[1] fourteen, where Shakespeare has thirty-one. The average number of speaking characters in Restoration tragedy is not more than fourteen, not much more than half the usual number in Shakespeare. The confinement of the character element in the later drama within a circumscribed compass is, then, patent. Attention is concentrated on a smaller picture, and the search for Elizabethan multifariousness is futile. It is claimed that a limited vocabulary possesses a peculiar strength, and it might be inferred that the stream of energy is the same in either case; that it is merely a question whether to allow it to flow over a wide expanse or to confine it in a narrower channel, thus intensifying its force; that the change from many characters to a less number brings about a closer attention, and hence a

[1] "Antony and Cleopatra." By Sir Charles Sedley. 1677.

more careful consideration of the remainder; that what these characters lack in variety they make up in quality. Whether or not in the abstract this assumption be permissible, it is certainly unwarrantable in its present connection. The characters that were drawn, and that were in a sense so popular as to be many times repeated or imitated, are not comparable to the figures of the older time.

Did the Restoration dramatists fail in character delineation through inability, or rather because they had another object in view than the painting of men and women, and purposely relegated that part of their work to an unimportant place, if they did not disregard it entirely? What, in its relation to character, was the intent of the heroic play? Not surely to paint men as they are in the flesh; such an assertion was but a form of flattering the audience.

"Tis ten to one but th' Author still will say,
Your vertues were the patterns of his play;
And swear you down,
His Love and Honour both were stol'n from you;
And from your features he his Heroes drew.
There's ne'er a Comick Writer but will say,
You're all of you the patterns of his Play;

> Yet takes your pictures at so damn'd a light;
> Paints you so ugly that your looks would fright.
> Why in your hearts may not th' Heroicks share?
> Those make you worse, these better than you are.
> And flatt'rers sure should not successless prove,
> When those that do abuse you have your love." [1]

But it was the business of the heroic drama, as of other forms of tragedy, to paint men "better than they are"; and the distinction between the Elizabethan and the later manner was not one of observance of the dictum, but of interpretation. Hamlet thinks deeper and feels more keenly than an everyday man; but the operation of his mind and heart is thoroughly normal, in that it is perfectly human. In no regard is it superhuman. In all cases the Shakespearean meaning of painting a man better than others or superior to others is spiritual as opposed to physical and material; the accentuation of certain purely human qualities is what constitutes the Shakespearean hero; how much land he owns, or how much muscular strength he has, does not matter. There is verbal evidence also of the spiritual

[1] "Ibrahim, the Illustrious Bassa." By Elkanah Settle. 1677. Epilogue.

aspect, in Restoration drama, of the elemental passions, greatly overcolored, to be sure.

"Love rages in great souls,
For there his power most opposition finds;
High trees are shook, because they dare the winds."[1]

It is taken for granted that only in the higher spheres of life is the exaltation of love and war possible:

"The lover and the brave
Are ranked, at least, above the vulgar slave;"[2]

and also of prudence and the sense of glory, —

"Where is that harmony of mind, that prudence,
Which guided all you did? that sense of glory,
Which raised you high above the rest of kings,
As kings are o'er the level of mankind?"[3]

In the last two lines may be found the key to the first point of departure from the Shakespearean standard in post-Elizabethan and Carolean art, — an attempt at first not so much to introduce new features as to magnify through exaggeration certain human qualities to an extent hitherto untried and unprecedented, and soon pushed to the impossible because

[1] "Secret Love, or the Maiden Queen." By John Dryden. 1668. Act 2, Sc. 1.

[2] "Conquest of Granada," Part 2, Act 4, Sc. 3.

[3] "Maiden Queen," Act 2, Sc. 1.

beyond nature. The extravagance of the later Elizabethan and early post-Elizabethan drama, begun in Shakespeare's own day, suggests whither things were drifting; but the tendency does not appear to have been formulated, recognized, and championed as a laudable principle till Dryden wrote that "the laws of an heroic poem" justified "drawing all things as far above the ordinary proportion of the stage as that is beyond the common words and actions of human life."[1] Magnifying all things did not lead to a nicer and subtler working-over of old material, but to an illegitimate introduction of new things; it encouraged extraneousness, put a premium on the irrelevant, and distracted attention from the character itself to physical qualities and to material wealth. The idea was old on the Continent, but its application was an innovation in English dramatic literature. Dryden endeavors to justify from history his treatment of physical prowess:

"But we have read both of Cæsar, and many other generals, who have not only calmed a mutiny with a word, but have presented them-

[1] John Dryden, "Essay on Heroic Plays." 1672.

selves single before an army of their enemies; which upon sight of them has revolted from their own leaders, and come over to their trenches. If the history of the late Duke of Guise be true, he hazarded more and performed not less in Naples, than Almanzor is feigned to have done in Granada."[1]

The physical properties of a hero are marvellous. He is indeed a full-blooded person:

"Let the blind Queen of Chance her Envy shew,
And save thy life by some successless blow;
Deny'd all help, and pass'd defence withstood,
I'll rip my breast, and drown thee with my blood."[2]

Combating single-handed an army or two is but a mild form of pleasant recreation; and

"Those few million we've yet vanquish't are
A bare dumb shew of a poor pageant war."[3]

But the strangest feature of his strength is that it does not leave the body with death, but his ghost continues the even tenor of his muscular way.

"If Souls can fight, I thee to Battle dare,
And mine shall hence only to meet thee there."[4]

[1] Dryden, "Essay on Heroic Plays."
[2] "Siege of Memphis," Act 1, Sc. 2.
[3] "Conquest of China," Act 1, Sc. 1.
[4] "Herod and Mariamne." By Samuel Pordage. 1673. Act 5, Sc. 7.

"Revenging still, and following ev'n to the other
world my blow;
And shoving this earth on which I sit,
I'll mount and scatter all the Gods I hit."[1]

Worldly possessions as an attribute of majesty is frequently the opening theme of a play. Thus begins Weston's "Amazon Queen":

"'Tis time our King leave his bold chace of Fame,
Now nothing more can add to his great name;
He has no foes like great Darius left,
Whom he of more than half the world bereft."[2]

And thus Banks's "Rival Kings":

"From Ganges, and beyond Nyle's secret Bed,
Strange conquer'd nations have *Euphrates* spread,
By Heaven's eternal power ordained to meet
In the World's center, and its Royal seat.
From other Parts whilest succours bend their course,
You bring from *Greece*, the Foot to re-inforce,
And I from *Thrace*, five thousand Winged horse.
So the great Sea maintains its swelling Pride
By lesser streams that thither daily glide;
All things contribute to this mighty King,
To *Alexander* flowing, leave their Spring,
And aids from the remotest places bring."[3]

1 "Tyrannic Love, or the Royal Martyr." By John Dryden. 1670. Act 5, Sc. 1.
2 "Amazon Queen," Act 1, Sc. 1.
3 "Rival Kings," Act 1, Sc. 1.

Greater than this is to come:

> "The Conquerours of *Persia*, *Macedon*,
> The Lords of Cæsars reverence my Throne;
> Clear from the rising to the setting sun;
> What *Alexander* ne'er could reach, I won."

And he is answered:

> "Sir, from *Japan* to the *Atlantic* Main,
> The World lies fetter'd in your glorious chain
> Whose Light and Influence in the Heavens is felt,
> As upon Earth the spangled Milky belt." [1]

And himself proclaims:

> "Had *Cæsar* liv'd I had taught that Rebel Peace;
> And lash'd the stragling Demi-God to *Greece*." [2]

And —

> "The trembling World has shook at my alarms,
> *Asia* and *Africa* have felt my arms.
> My glorious Conquests too did farther flye;
> I taught the *Egyptian* god Mortality;
> By me great Apis fell, and now you see
> They are compelled to change their gods for me.
> I have done deeds, where Heaven's high pow'r was foyl'd.
> Piercing those Rocks where Thunder has been toyl'd.
> Now, like our sun, when there remains no more,
> Thither return whence we set out before."

[1] "Sacrifice," Act 1, Sc. 1.
[2] *Ibid.*

"*Otan.* Returning thus, Great Sir, you have out-done
All other glories, which your arms have won.
Inferiour Conquerours their Triumphs get
When they advance, but you when you retreat.
Dar. All Worthies now must yield to you alone,
And disappear as stars before the Sun.
Thus *Cyrus*, who all *Asia* did defeat,
Because so near you, does not seem so great.
Prex. Cambyses, no; Your Honour there must yield;
Your father Cyrus's fame has yours excell'd
Since in one act he did all yours out-do,
In leaving such a glorious Son as you." [1]

But if Caligula be as truthful as he is hopeful, he certainly of all rulers had the greatest domain:

"I reign from Heav'n to hell; — perhaps beyond." [2]

The exaggeration of human qualities and the introduction of externals were intended, doubtless, to increase the "illustriousness," as it were, of the character; to make the hero more heroic, to delineate him as "perfect pattern of heroic virtues," [3] and pattern "of exact virtues." [4] The word "pattern" — anything proposed for imitation, or what is itself made after a model — thrice employed by Dryden in description of

[1] "Cambyses," Act 1, Sc. 1. [2] "Caligula," Act 4.
[3] Dryden, "Essay on Heroic Plays." [4] *Ibid.*

his own creations, indicates the absence of individualization; it presupposes, invites, and facilitates the process of classification. There was little or no attempt to draw men and women, but rather to present abstract human qualities. There is further evidence in Langbaine's remark on Orrery's dramatic works, where attention is called to the quality depicted rather than to the personality of the character. In them, he writes, is "true English courage delineated to the life."[1] From Otway's words also it is plain that the hero was looked upon as the embodiment of heroic virtues, and the dramatist considered their quality and quantity rather than — and at the expense of — personality.

> "I durst presume to put this poem under your patronage . . . for . . . the mighty encouragement I have received from your approbation of it when presented on the stage was hint enough to let me know at whose feet it ought to be laid. Yet, . . . I am sensible the curious world will expect some panegyric on those heroic virtues which are throughout it so much admired."[2]

[1] Langbaine, p. 27.

[2] "Don Carlos, Prince of Spain." By Thomas Otway. 1676. Dedication.

The lack of diversity in the types has been contrasted with Shakespearean richness. The exuberance of character of the Elizabethan stage passed away. The mirror of life held up to nature, re-creating the human family in all its phases of mental and moral development, of rank and fortune, was exchanged for another of different make and for a different purpose. The play-scene was robbed of its wealth, left poor and comparatively bare. Impoverishment was brought about by the extensive reduction in the number of characters, with its attendant omission of certain phases of life exemplified in certain creations, and by the transformation or substitution, or both, of the remainder. For the stage was far poorer than the mere cutting down by half, or even more, of Shakespearean characters would have left it, if the other half had remained in nature Shakespearean. Shakespeare never duplicates characters. But the Restoration dramatists frequently copied theirs. The characters became conventionalized to such an extent as to be but faintly distinguishable one from another. This obviously rendered the stage poorer than it would have been simply through omissions.

The heroic drama proper admitted no comic element and excluded all classes of society except the nobility. This wholesale process of exclusion did away with the clown in his various rôles, and all smile-evoking wit; and under the latter head representatives of the people and mobs (pageants were retained, but no mobs), all trades-people, — in brief, whatsoever in the exact sense was uncourtly; and intellectually and emotionally, all characters of introspection and true passion.[1]

The leading type of the heroic play may be seen in Antony, Richmond, and Henry V., as drawn by Sedley, Caryl, and Orrery, but Almanzor is more complete, depicted with greater detail and more brilliantly. Therefore a rehearsal of his characteristics seems desirable, especially as he is the acknowledged example, *par excellence*, of the kind he represents, — the "echte blume,"[2] as Holzhausen calls him, of the heroic manner, and its "most complete expression in Dryden."[3] His first entrance indicates the manner of man. The first line shows his entire indifference to justice; he has no idea of right and wrong.

[1] See Appendix B. [2] Holzhausen, E. S., xiii. 432.
[3] *Ibid.* xv. 44.

The second discloses a desire to relieve the oppressed, — a desire, however, without depth or catholicity. He rushes on the stage where there are two men ready to engage, and separates them with these words:

> "I cannot stay to ask which cause is best;
> But this is so to me because opprest."[1]

He next describes a line with his sword and forbids trespassing.

> "Upon thy life pass not this middle space;
> Sure death stands guarding the forbidden place."[2]

Here is the modern melodramatic hero, — the "halt-or-I-shoot" sort. He is dared, kills, is disarmed, and threatened with death. He replies that he scorns life, but denies the right of any one but himself to take it away.

[1] "Conquest of Granada," Pt. 1, Act 1, Sc. 1. Cf. "Don Carlos" (Act 4, Sc. 1), who, when asked if he will go over to the rebels, replies:

> "No, they're friends; their cause is just;
> Or, when I make it mine, at least it must."

[2] *Ibid.* Perhaps the most familiar illustration of this device is the "magic circle" in Bulwer's "Richelieu." There is no doubt of its theatrical effectiveness.

"But know that I alone am king of me,
I am as free as nature first made man,
Ere the base laws of servitude began,
When wild in woods the noble savage ran,"[1]

and nonchalantly defies the death sentence:

"Stand off, I have not leisure yet to die."[2]

He has previously told the king that they ought to change positions, — *i.e.* that he himself should "in nature" have the throne.

"I saw the oppressed, and thought it did belong
To a king's office to redress the wrong;
I brought that succour which thou oughtst to bring,
And so, in nature, am thy subjects' king."[3]

This passage also reveals a leaning to sophistry, — to "argumentation in verse," as Dr. Garnett puts it, — chronic with Dryden, and common among his fellows.

Almanzor is thus described:

"Vast is his courage, boundless is his mind,
Rough as a storm and humorous as wind;

[1] "Conquest of Granada," Pt. 1, Act 1, Sc. 1. The doctrine of the "return to nature," popularly associated with Rousseau, was by no means an uncommon note in English Restoration literature. For other instances in prose and verse, see Mrs. Behn's "Oroonoko," 1668, *passim*, and Otway's "Don Carlos," Act 2.

[2] *Ibid.* [3] *Ibid.*

Honour's the only idol of his eyes;
The charms of beauty, like a pest, he flies;
And raised by valour from a birth unknown
Acknowledges no power above his own."[1]

His courage is indeed vast; it is prodigious. He is also humorous as the wind, — capricious, admitting no law superior to himself. Honor, such as it was, is somewhat in evidence. Practically, however, it is about as deep as the desire to help the oppressed. But the whole description gives a very incomplete picture, and the line about running away from the charms of beauty is misleading, because it omits the very quiddity of the character, if it stands for the type, for, above all else, he is a lover. His true identity (not his birth) is then made known to the king, who revokes the sentence and asks his aid. The king addresses his subjects and is unheeded, whereupon Almanzor speaks and all obey his bidding. They do this so readily that he has a chance to indulge his contempt for the common people.

"Hence, you unthinking crowd!
Empire, thou poor and despicable thing,
When such as these make or unmake a king!"[2]

[1] *Ibid.* [2] *Ibid.*

Such is his thought, but the wonder of his action impresses the by-standers.

> " How much of virtue lies in one great soul,
> Whose single force can multitudes control ! " [1]

Almanzor bids his new-found friends not to worry, because

> " The Moors have heaven and me t' assist their cause." [2]

He comes on the stage with the Duke of Arcos, the Moors' enemy, a prisoner, and says he will set him free, in order that he may fight him again, for he enjoys fighting.

> " It pleases me your army is so great;
> For now I know there's more to conquer yet.
>
> * * * * * * *
>
> I'll go, and instantly acquaint the king,
> And sudden orders for thy freedom bring.
> Thou canst not be so pleased at liberty
> As I shall be to find thou darest be free." [3]

This the king refuses to do, which puts Almanzor in an agreeable mood to hearken to Abdalla, the king's brother, and aspirant to the throne.

[1] " Conquest of Granada," Pt. 1, Act 1, Sc. 1.
[2] *Ibid.*
[3] *Ibid.* Pt. 1, Act 2, Sc. 1.

"When I show my title you shall see
I have a better right to reign than he."[1]

Almanzor straightway declares himself Abdalla's friend, and his friendship is like his helping the weaker side, it disregards title and justice.

"It is sufficient that you make the claim;
You wrong our friendship when your right you name.
When for myself I fight, I weigh the cause,
But friendship will admit of no such laws;

* * * * * * *

True, I would wish my friend the juster side;
But, in the unjust, my kindness more is tried."[2]

"For you to will, for me 'tis to obey."[3]

In the first love scene between the principal characters both fall in love at first sight, the lover more noticeably, and he is affected in the conventional manner.

"I fear it is the lethargy of love!
'Tis he; I feel him now in every part;
Like a new lord he vaunts about my heart;

* * * * * * *

I'm all o'er love;
Nay, I am love; love shot, and shot so fast
He shot himself into my breast at last."[4]

[1] *Ibid.* Pt. 1, Act 3, Sc. 1. [2] *Ibid.* [3] *Ibid.* [4] *Ibid.*

His behavior in its formalism and elaboration would appear to discredit his own words:

> "'Tis the essay of an untaught first love." [1]

But it is difficult in more ways than one to regard him as he regards himself.

> "But all court customs I so little know," [2]

he says. Once before he has suggested a likeness between himself and "the noble savage." He is a quibbler, and the fact that Almahide is already contracted to Boabdelin disconcerts him but a moment.

> "I bring a claim which does his right remove;
> You're his by promise, but you're mine by love.
> 'Tis all but ceremony which is past;
> The knot's to tie which is to make you fast.
> Fate gave not to Boabdelin that power;
> He wooed you but as my ambassador." [3]

She is his captive by the right of war, but he disdains to keep her, and declares her free;

[1] "Conquest of Granada," Pt. 1, Act 3, Sc. 1.
[2] *Ibid.* Pt. 2, Act 5, Sc. 2. [3] *Ibid.*

and when asked if such action does not show generosity but also lack of love, he replies,

> " 'Tis exalted passion, when I show
> I dare be wretched not to make her so;"[1]

and that he had rather be entirely wretched than half blest while another passion fills her heart.

He next meets Abdalla, and has an opportunity to practise the friendship which be has already expounded. But when he learns Abdalla loves Almahide, all friendship disappears; and because Abdalla does not yield, Almanzor thinks him ungrateful and himself wronged, and so returns to the other side, and explains his shifting thus:

> "Great souls by kindness only can be tied;
> Injured again, again I'll leave your side."[2]

Almanzor has told Almahide that she is at liberty. Just as his behavior belied his principles in loyalty and friendship, so when asked again if she is free, he answers,

> "Madam, you are, from all the world,—but me!"

[1] *Ibid.* [2] *Ibid.* Pt. 1, Act 4, Sc. 1.
[3] *Ibid.* Pt. 1, Act 4, Sc. 2.

She yields willingly to be his, if she can do so with propriety ; but she asks her lover to carry himself a little more humbly, with not quite so much fierceness. He comforts her by saying that he can beg when the time requires, but really the time never does require. If, in order to make her father perfectly content with the match, nothing but a country to rule over is wanted, matters can be easily arranged.

> "And if your father will require a crown,
> Let him but name the kingdom, 'tis his own."[1]

He is but remaining for the time being a private man only because he wants to do so, for he says he has "that soul which empires first began," consequently,

> "The best and bravest souls I can select,
> And on their conquered necks my throne erect."[2]

He admits he

> "Twice has changed for wrongs received,"[3]

but defends his haughtiness against his love's suggestion to moderate it.

[1] "Conquest of Granada," Pt. 1, Act 4, Sc. 2.
[2] *Ibid.* [3] *Ibid.* Pt. 2, Act 3, Sc. 3.

"If I am proud, 'tis only to my foes;
Rough but to such who virtue would oppose.
If I some fierceness from a father drew,
A mother's milk gives me some softness too." [1]

When it is rumored that Almahide is false and the emperor raves, Almanzor assures him that a husband's honor is not so important as a lover's and that himself has more cause for grievance. He questions her constancy, but what Dryden would doubtless call his "confidence of himself" comes to his rescue.

"She must be chaste, because she's loved by me." [2]

He still doubts, nevertheless, and is urged for his own honor's sake to keep up appearances.

"Yet her protection I must undertake;
Not now for love, but for my honour's sake
That moved me first." [3]

In his way he remains true to Almahide. Once he became overbold and was deterred only by a threat that she would kill herself. "And what is honour," he asks, "but a love well hid?"

[1] *Ibid.* [2] *Ibid.* Pt. 2, Act 4, Sc. 3.
[3] *Ibid.* Pt. 2, Act 5, Sc. 1.

> "Praise is the pay of heaven for doing good;
> But love's the best return for flesh and blood." [1]

The emperor is killed in battle, Almahide goes into a year's mourning, offering hope to Almanzor at its expiration. His birth is discovered, and Almahide and a throne await him.

The author thus analyzes his creation:

"I have formed a hero, I confess, not absolutely perfect, but of an excessive and overboiling courage; but Homer and Tasso are my precedents. . . .

"But a character of an eccentric virtue is the more exact image of human life, because he is not wholly exempted from its frailties; such a person is Almanzor. . . . I designed in him roughness of character, impatient of injuries, and a confidence of himself, almost approaching to an arrogance. But these errors are incident only to great spirits; they are moles and dimples which hinder not a face from being beautiful, though that beauty be not regular. . . . And such in Almanzor are a frank and noble openness of nature, an easiness to forgive his conquered enemies, and to protect them in distress; and, above all, an inviolable faith in his affection. . . . Heroes should only be judged by heroes, because they only are capable of measuring great and heroic actions by the rule and standard of their own."

[1] "Conquest of Granada," Pt. 2, Act 4, Sc. 3.

The dramatist concludes, indirectly asking the reader to believe that Almanzor does not fail in any "point of honour," and that "he fulfils the parts of personal valour, and of conduct of a soldier and of a general."[1]

It should perhaps be added in justice to Dryden's dramatic feeling that later in life he repented him of this character.[2] Even at this time he was not nearly so mightily impressed with him as he would have the detractors believe. He was conscious of insincerity, which is amusingly suggested by his confession as to the true nature of Almanzor's bravery. "After all," he says, "the greatness of the enterprize consisted only in the daring, for he had the king's guards to second him."[3]

Love is the main theme of all heroic plays, and the sole theme of many. All major and most minor characters are lovers. A consideration of them as such is the only one that the playwright permits himself. The hero is always a warrior, but the martial element is made so

[1] *Ibid.* Dedication.

[2] "Spanish Friar, or the Double Discovery." By John Dryden. 1681. Dedication.

[3] Dryden, "Essay on Heroic Plays."

unimportant that nought but the lover remains. Lack of complexity and of individualization makes a citation of several characters unnecessary. It is, indeed, in this lack of true characterization and interest in other passions than love that the absence of Shakespearean variety is manifested quite as much as in the entire omission of certain forms. A description of the leading character of a Shakespearean play answers no other ; but Almanzor is well-nigh a complete embodiment of all the qualities that the corresponding figures of other heroic plays possess.

The general statement may be qualified to a certain extent by a treatment of the villain, because the individuals of the type differ from one another more than individual heroes differ from each other. As an indication of the greater stress put upon love than upon ambition, the latter quality, which has been of good repute in the actual world of all time, is practised and extolled in the heroic drama only by the villains.

> "In sluggish Breasts Love's idle frenzy rules ;
> Ambition is the Lust of all great Souls." [1]

[1] "Conquest of China," Act 3, Sc. 3.

It is not until the third act that Lycurgus asks for an audience to behold his courage, savagery, fierceness, and boldness.

> "Ye Gods of *China*, if you are such tame
> And inoffensive things, as our *Priests* frame,
> Whose Pious Eares and Eyes and tender Sense
> Delights in nought but Good and Innocence;
> Draw back your Sun, and vele yourselves in night;
> I shall Act Deeds, which all weak Eyes will fright.
> But if the Nature of your God-Heads be
> Courageous, savage, fierce and bold like me,
> Heav'n wear no Clouds, and Gods take a full view;
> Look and admire at what my Hand dares doe." [1]

In his case, ambition is unalloyed with any other passion. He is slave to no woman.

> "Who, but a loving fool,
> Wou'd damn his own to save a woman's Soul"? [2]

He is one of the very few conspicuous figures of the heroic drama that devotes practically no attention to them. In him also the desire to be a warrior is plainly marked, though the end of war is but to achieve power. His very first words show his inclination to be head of the army rather than of internal affairs.

> "A Gown's not that my soaring wishes want;
> The Sword had been the more obliging grant." [3]

[1] *Ibid.* [2] *Ibid.* Act 4, Sc. 2. [3] *Ibid.* Act 2.

When his usurpation of the throne is temporarily successful, he says:

> "No; *China's* Crown has 'till my Reign been worn
> By lazy Kings, with Female Spirits born;
> Guarded by Eunuchs, bred in Palaces,
> Nurtur'd in Lusts, the Progeny of Peace;
> But now's the time, Fate grants the High Command
> Of this Great Empire to a Martial Hand!" [1]

There is a slight love element in Melynet's life, but it is unimportant. He thus chooses a villanous career for the sake of power over the king.

"It is only being blest by Fortune in the end, that gives the intention value. That's the unjust scale, by which the world weighs all things. But why should I condemn ingratitude as Vice, that for ambition turn a Villain and betray my friend? Yet 'tis not I am guilty, though I act the Crime; 'tis the abusive world which throws such heaps of injuries and scorns on wanting Virtue, that mans courage cannot bear it; at least mine shall not, if a streach'd conscience will relieve me.

> "I'll grasp a fortune though I heav'n let go,
> That I have heard of, but 'tis this I know;" [2]

[1] "Conquest of China," Act 5.
[2] "Marcelia," Act 1, Sc. 6.

He repents in this manner:

"Vain joys of mortal Life! you fly so fast
Man hardly knows you are before you're past;
Yet we on you do our affections lay,
As if we here eternally should stay.
Honor, thou now dost give my soul a view
Of what I left when first I banish'd you.
O Virtue! how have I bin led astray,
From thy fair paths, into this Lab'rynth way?
I thought my fortune on a rock did stand,
But Guilts foundation still proves foolish sand.
When man by Crimes does plots for greatness lay,
Heav'n justly frowns and takes his hopes away.
But though my life bears characters of shame;
My death shall leave behind a better Fame." [1]

Revenge for wrongs and unsuccessful love is Jasper's excuse. "Fatal Jealousie" is, strictly speaking, only partly a heroic play; the amount of rhyme is small, and the character range is comparatively large. But Jasper is one of the most interesting villains of Restoration tragedy. He tells his own story:

"*Capt.* For what should move thee to this Villainy?
Jasp. For that you will not wonder.
I am *Jasper de Monsalvo*, Heir to that Estate
This Lord doth now possess.
Anto. Ah Heav'ns! some of that desperate Bandity
Did once attempt my life.

[1] *Ibid.* Act 5, Sc. 8.

Jasp. Yes truly. . . .

Anto. Poor *Celia*, 'tis no wonder thy mind did boad
Great mischiefs from this Fellow, being Son of
One did still contrive to kill me, for what the
King after just forfeiture for mighty services
Had given my Father.

Jasp. O Revenge!
Thy sweetness takes away the taste of Death.
But you'l lose my story; which in short is this:
That Lady lov'd me not, and therefore I
Made her Lord Jealous, took him to a Witch,
And there I fool'd him finely: till the Jade,
Who was my Aunt indeed, at your approach
Would have discover'd all; which I prevented,
And stopt her Mouth with this: Then I contriv'd
To kill *Eugenia*, knowing she would meet
Francisco in the Garden; that I did
Because she call'd me Villain, and refus'd
To let me Whore her too, as did her Couzen;
And more, I knew the simple Lord I serv'd
When he had murder'd her, as I should make him,
Would thank my Care, and well reward it too:
Nay, I'd have him do't for his own safety,
That still the Murder might be thought *Francisco's;*
You know the rest i' th' Garden. I taught besides
That damn'd Old Hagg, whose fear has made me thus,
To put this trick on *Pedro;* I bid her call him
When she should hear us whistle, then in haste,
And all undrest send him to *Celia's* Chamber,
Whilst we, let in, might meet him coming thence,
Thinking the Cuckold's Rage would murder all,
And never hear 'em speak; but there I fail'd,
Their dying words betray'd me, that's the worst,

Or I had liv'd to glory in their Deaths;
But this my Comfort is, he'l not survive me,
I have done his bus'ness too before I dye.
Sevv. Was er'e so impudent a Villain seen?
Capt. I'le try to stop his wounds, that so
I may keep him for Execution.
Jasp. Stand off, by Hell,
He that comes near me finds his Death with this!
Think you I'm grown so tame to dye by Law;
No, no I'le not endure a formal Tryal,
To be upbraided with those things I think
Deserve a Trophy rather than Contempt,
Which since I know will follow, here's my bail,
This will deliver any Man from Jayl.
Let Cowards dye by hanging; such as I
As we live bravely, thus dare bravely dye.
[*Stabs himself.*" [1]

This account does not even suggest the wit, vivacity, and sprightliness shown in scenes which lose their virtue in description but which make the character memorable, and which doubtless put Baker in mind of a Shakespearean prototype.[2] The comparison, of course, was very unfavorable, but the mere fact that any resemblance was seen is really praise.

[1] "Fatal Jealousie," Act 5.

[2] David Erskine Baker, "Biographia Dramatica, or a Companion to the Playhouse." 1811. ii. 229. "The character of Jasper seems to be a bad copy of Iago in 'Othello.'"

Richard is swayed both by ambition and love. He is a "tyrant," and Richmond a "lover." The first term probably means "a cruel ruler," and Richard with his past crimes and present threats against the life of the princess deserves the title. Many heroic villains are tyrants; but it should be observed that being a villain or a tyrant does not prevent one from being a lover; rather love is the customary channel for exercising and explaining villany. Here, for example, in spite of their appellations, Richard is a lover as well as a tyrant. The lover is morally good and the tyrant bad, but in essentials, — desire for success in war and love, — they are alike, and there is no complexity in either. There is no harmony between the sentiments and those who voice them. Richard, for example, complains thus :

> "With Patience, like Love's Martyr, I have born
> Not only her Denials, but her Scorn." [1]

"Geneste observes (of Crowne's Caligula) that the author has 'been very injudicious in the choice of his subject — it was not possible to construct a good play on the story of Caligula — he was a monster of wickedness, but none of

[1] "English Princess," Act 3, Sc. 2.

his actions was of such a nature as to produce a good effect upon the stage.' Had our author attempted to frame a dramatic chronicle of the life of this execrable tyrant, the critique might have been accepted, but this was not the object of the writer. Giving the piece the name of Caligula did not necessarily constitute him its hero. The name was used as a peg on which to hang the plot, and this has been done by Crowne with more success than might have been anticipated, when the circumstances under which the tragedy was written are taken into consideration." [1]

A great deal of space is devoted to an exposition of Caligula. He is on the stage much of the time, his speeches are long and frequent; and because of this, as the action is somewhat slow, his personality seems to dominate the whole. It is probably because of the slowness of the action — for the first two acts are consumed almost entirely with an exposition of his character and power — that the first impression is that a study in character has been attempted; [2]

[1] "The Dramatic Works of John Crowne," with memoir and notes by James Maidment and W. H. Logan. 1874. iv. 339.

[2] "Of this tragedy it will suffice to say, that though it reveals a praiseworthy attempt at character-drawing, the baldness of its form in general corresponds to the commonplace character of its sentiment." — Ward, iii. 403–404.

it continues to seem altogether too important to be styled merely "a peg on which to hang the plot."

Deriving from history sufficient information out of which to construct a character was a different matter from giving a character "as pourtrayed by"[1] the historian. Crowne did the former. There is no need of questioning his main source as Suetonius, and from him he could have derived a certain amount of biographical detail, seemingly considerable only because unusual, and also the framework of human monstrosity. But when Caligula had been successfully subjected to the requirements of a rhyming villain of the Restoration stage, he was necessarily transformed, and the likeness to the real emperor[2] or the emperor of the historians was much diminished. Not surely in this wise did the real emperor woo:

> "Goddess! — so, no doubt, you are,
> No mortal can be so divinely fair.

[1] "The Emperor is given as pourtrayed by Suetonius, upon whose scandalous, but — we suspect — tolerably correct biography, Crowne has drawn largely." — MAIDMENT and LOGAN, iv. 340.

[2] "Crowne has drawn the character of the Emperor according to history." — GENEST, ii. 143.

Nay, nay, at my request, sweet madam, rise;
Let all your graces entertain my eyes!
To Cæsar grant the infinite delight
To touch, and see a hand so soft and white.
Were all thy other beauties cheats of art,
This hand might palm a passion on my heart." [1]

It is difficult to dissociate the matter from the diction, but his mind was not given to "purling streams," even though it may have been to "pleasing dreams."

"The falls of nations, which fill cowards with fears
Shall but like water-falls delight our ears;
And murmuring subjects shall, like purling streams,
But lull us deeper in our pleasing dreams." [2]

Nor was the real character, according to Suetonius at all addicted to cynical meditation, and frequent discourses on his own greatness. It appears on study that, if there was an attempt made to reproduce the historical figure, it was not, from a strict test, successful; and there is not nearly the variety to the character that such an assumption would forecast. The banishment of most of the elements of life, with the comprisal only of the concernments of love and war, those passions being employed in their simplest and most literal way — love, to be

[1] "Caligula," Act 4. [2] *Ibid.* Act 1.

sure, somewhat formal yet for the most part physical, and war no more, no less, than combat on the battle-field — greatly narrowed the space for character display. So Caligula has much in common after all with the rank and file of heroic villains. In place of variety there is repetition. At the same time there remain enough points of contact between him and his historic prototype, — points moreover opposite to heroic tradition such as inconstancy in love — to differentiate him none the less clearly, because not wholly, from the others; and in degree, if not in kind, his villainy was deeper dyed and more monster-like. The character is almost motiveless. Revenge, ambition, disappointed love, do not account for his actions, but rather lust, desire for blood, innate depravity.

The hero is nearly always a young man, and the same is true of the villain; but there is generally an old man concerned, who may occupy a distinct, though not the principal, place; he may, indeed, be synonymous with the hero,[1] but more often he is allied with the villain element. Maximinian,[2] one of the most famous seventeenth-century characters,

[1] "Sacrifice." [2] "Tyrannic Love."

the emperor in the "Conquest of Granada," the two Herods,[1] Solyman in "Ibrahim," Solyman in "Mustapha,"[2] and Ibrahim in the "Conspiracy,"[3] are all old, and are all amorous. It may be the jealous husband, the doting father, the aged monarch; but they do not differ much from one another. Age does not bring with it individualization, to say nothing of discretion. A gray-haired and oft-married sultan uses the same language of extravagant enthusiasm, as soon as he sees the heroine, that a young lover would use.

A feature common to the plays is the character of the unsuccessful rival to the hero. He is sometimes a villain, perhaps the villain, who resorts to foul means to advance himself in his lady's regard, and is false to friendship. Such a villain is Altemast, who disguises himself as a woman, not for the gratification of lust, but to ingratiate himself into the heart of Altemira, and takes advantage of her confidence. Seleucus in "Tryphon" is a false friend.

[1] "Herod the Great." By Roger Boyle, Earl of Orrery. 1673. And "Herod and Mariamne."

[2] "Mustapha, the son of Solyman the Magnificent." By Roger Boyle, Earl of Orrery. 1668.

[3] "Conspiracy, or the Change of Government." By M. Whitaker. 1680.

"Our fortunes, Sir, with the like Malice move;
You love one sister; I the other love;
You have a rival who her heart has won,
To me my Rival the like Wrong has done;
But that at which we justly should repine,
Your Friend's your Rival, and my Friend is mine."[1]

He debates with himself and decides to prove false.

"Oh! whither by my Passion am I led?
My Love should die after my Hopes are dead;
She has herself declar'd to me that she
Has giv'n to him that which is sought by me;
Nor is Aretus guilty of the Crime;
He does to me what I'd have done to him;
Because in Love I cannot reach my End,
Why should Revenge deprive me of my Friend?
Great Gods! how can I prove so cold and tame,
As on a Rival to bestow that name?
And while Aretus does my joys ingross,
Talk myself into patience for my loss?
Since Friendship thus does plead for my Disgrace,
Revenge, do thou ascend, and take the Place;
Thou more like Virtue dost to me appear,
Than Friendship can, in this Affront I bear,
Since to the Brave nothing should be above
Revenge in Wrongs, or Constancy in Love;
Therefore thy Death, proud Rival, I'll pursue;
If I must lose her, thou must lose her too."[2]

For a time he exults in his guilt.

[1] "Tryphon," Act 5. [2] *Ibid.*

"You, ere I cou'd make you my great Request,
Told me, Aretus reigned within your Breast;
Ah! when I found that he was Monarch there,
I did, compell'd by Love and by Despair,
Discover all to Tryphon, with Design,
Helping his Love to make him further mine.
This, Madam, you may look on as my Sin;
But, what you think my guilt, I glory in;
For what more fully could my Passion prove,
Than sacrificing of my Friends to Love?" [1]

In the end, however, he admits to his successful rival the justice of his fate.

"Under such Loads of Guilt myself I find,
That I, tho' forc'd by Love, your Death design'd,
As I the greatest suff'rings ought to bear,
And therefore yield t' endure the loss of her." [2]

But among unsuccessful lovers there is many a true friend, and self-sacrifice is by no means infrequent. Tudor is perhaps the most comprehensive illustration; but Delaware, in "The Black Prince," and Sir William Stanley [3] are of a like nature, and in a humbler sphere the love of the servants and keepers above their rank, such as Hametalhaz in the "Empress of Morocco" [4] and Ulama in "Ibrahim."

[1] *Ibid.* [2] *Ibid.* [3] English Princess.
[4] "Empress of Morocco." By Elkanah Settle. 1673.

The friend and rival are frequently the same among principal personages, but in the lesser figures the friend merges into the confidant, and the confidant, although in every play, is utterly without distinction.

Although the combination of friendship and rivalry is common among men, it is exceedingly rare among women. The case of the two Amazons, who, until a lover made them rivals, had lived in the closest friendship, and then vieing to outdo each other in generosity eventually decided to share him successive years, though minor, seems to be the only one in point.[1]

The heroine of this kind of drama falls in love with the hero usually at first sight, as soon after the opening of the play as possible, if she is not already in that state. She is young and beautiful, though her beauty is never tangibly described except that her eyes are irresistible. She may be either maid, wife, or widow, at the time of the hero's advent; but if she be wife, she remains true to her husband, although his jealousy may bring about her death. But she admits her love for the hero, and he finds oppor-

[1] "Amazon Queen," Act 4, Sc. 1.

tunities to make his addresses. The story of their love is a primary matter of the play, and she is not interested in any other concern. Holzhausen's remark that women in Dryden understand how to philosophize about passion, but themselves are devoid of feeling,[1] may be extended to his contemporaries and successors in playwriting.

The Maiden Queen has been praised among Dryden's women,[2] and she embodies, moreover, many of the typical traits. She has the traditional anti-democratic sentiment regarding the peoples' rights as compared with her own,[3] and a dislike of being ruled by a husband, especially one imposed upon her,[4] with a touch of cynical worldliness on the power of gold to win affection.

> "All eyes are fair,
> That sparkle with the jewels of a crown." [5]

Her counsellors advise her to marry. As soon as the "factious deputies" are gone, she stands alone in the presence of the man she loves, who knows it not. This scene is marked by a certain attention to the mood.

[1] Holzhausen, E. S., xiii. 435. [2] Pepys.
[3] "Maiden Queen," Act 1, Sc. 3. [4] *Ibid.* [5] *Ibid.*

She fluctuates, desiring him first to stay, then to go, then again to stay,[1] and weeps because he of all men urged her marriage,[2] and bemoans her want of freedom to love where she will.

> "Shall I, — I, who was born a sovereign queen,
> Be barred of that which God and nature gives
> The merest slave, a freedom in my love?"[3]

He reluctantly leaves her in her "high displeasure," accidentally dropping a picture, which is handed her. It is of Candiope, Prince Lysimantes' sister. She is angry at the revelation, and straightway remarks on the ugliness of the original, though rumor holds Candiope beyond comparison the fairest lady our isle can boast.[4] The queen, on being reminded of the change that has come over her disposition, says it does not matter, for her life will shortly be at an end. This leads to a confession of her love to a confidant and a planning between them as to how Philocles' love may be turned from Candiope unto herself; whether or not to prevent by "sovereign authority" the marriage of Candiope and Philocles.[5] There is a repetition of her indecision as to how to behave in the

[1] "Maiden Queen," Act 1, Sc. 3.
[2] *Ibid.* [3] *Ibid.* [4] *Ibid.* [5] *Ibid.*

presence of Philocles. She tells him she loves a man as worthy as himself, and then because he, in his ignorance, condemns such a man, she rebukes him and banishes him her presence, — for the day, — and herself resolves no more to love him.[1] Then, because her confidant agrees with her, she reproves the woman, saying,

> "I love him, and may rail; in you 'tis malice;"[2]

but soon repents.[3] It is not long before she meets her lover. He would run away, to avert her displeasure; for he has been banished; but she has forgotten all about it.[4]

The queen comes upon Candiope and her lover, is maddened at the sight, insults Candiope, detailing her physical imperfections, and finally, when Candiope rashly says,

> "What my faults are is no matter;
> He loves me with them all, —"

she retorts:

> "Ay, he may love; but when he marries you,
> Your bridal shall be kept in some dark dungeon.
> Farewell, and think of that, too easy maid.
> I blush thou sharest my blood."[5]

[1] *Ibid.* Act 2, Sc. 1. [2] *Ibid.* [3] *Ibid.*
[4] *Ibid.* Act 3, Sc. 1. [5] *Ibid.*

She goes out, but returns before the lovers have finished their scene, and from above listens to their wooing, hears herself called cruel, despises herself for still loving, and resolves anew to cease. She overhears them plotting an elopement, decides to ordain fitting punishment, and bids her attendant never to mention Philocles' name again.[1] The queen next commands the same woman to do nothing else but speak of Philocles, and classes herself with mad people who never think the same thing twice. She is between anger and love. Philocles has turned against her; she finds her power gone, but realizes virtue

> "Has but given me a great occasion
> Of showing what I am, when fortune leaves me."[2]

On being reminded that her lover is against her she answers with unwonted sincerity and naturalness:

> "Ay, Philocles! I must confess 'twas hard."[3]
>
> "Never till now unhappy queen."[4]

Asteria, unknown to her, indicates to Philocles the queen's love for him. The queen sus-

[1] "Maiden Queen," Act 3, Sc. 1.
[2] *Ibid.* Act 4, Sc. 2.
[3] *Ibid.*
[4] *Ibid.*

pects as much, and blames not more her confidant's "female weakness" than her own in trusting her. "O, whither am I fallen?" she says. But she determines upon a course of action — to rouse herself from her passion —

> "In hearts resolved weak love is put to flight,
> And only conquers, when we dare not fight."[1]

Lysimantes enters, he who has made her virtually a prisoner. He asks her hand in marriage, and is spurned. He upbraids her with loving beneath her. At the first suspicion that this love is known the queen says, in an aside:

> "This is the extremest malice of my stars."[2]

He accuses her plainly, mentions her jealousy of Candiope, and concludes,

> "Prove you love him not, yet give her him,
> And I'll engage my honour to lay down my arms.
> Now hold my heart, for this one act of honour,
> And I will never ask more courage of thee."[3]

And she believes her love shrinking and giving way to glory. But on the sight of Philocles she knows her passion is not banished, but only "chained up."[4] Yet she renounces her love,

[1] *Ibid.* Act 5, Sc. 1. [2] *Ibid.* [3] *Ibid.* [4] *Ibid.*

bids Philocles take Candiope, wishes them happiness, and is pleased with herself that she can force her tongue to speak words so distant from her heart; and for herself resolves to continue unmarried, and to devote her life to her subjects.[1] Lysimantes, who loves her, in imitation of her oath, vows a single life, and the play ends with her in complete joy, for the right of Lysimantes will devolve upon Candiope, and therefore will be

> "This great content, to think when I am dead,
> My crown may fall on Philocles head."

The Maiden Queen's actions have been thus specifically detailed because mainly through them is her character disclosed, and her character is of special importance because of Dryden's explicit statement: "It was as much as I designed, to show one great and absolute pattern of honour in my poem, which I did in the person of the queen; all the defects of the other parts being set to show, the more to recommend that one character of virtue to the audience."[2]

The Maiden Queen is painted with a little

[1] "Maiden Queen," Act 5, Sc. 1. [2] *Ibid.* Preface.

finer brush than most of the corresponding characters. It is the attention to the passing mood that distinguishes the delineation, and self-sacrifice is the most important element in her character. This quality is not typical to a noticeable extent of the virtuous women of the heroic drama, but through it a few of them deserve mention. Perhaps the queen herself is the only major character of the kind; the minor in Dryden is Amalthea in "Marriage-a-la-Mode," hieing to a nunnery and submitting to the pangs of unrequited love.

Asteria is the daughter of Solyman the Magnificent in "Ibrahim." Ibrahim is the sultan's favorite, and returning from victorious wars, is rewarded by Asteria's hand. Her love for him is unrequited, for he is betrothed to "Isabella, a Christian Princess," and at the risk of disgrace declines the sultan's offer. Isabella appears and Solyman becomes enamoured of her. Asteria, instead of scorning Ibrahim for evermore, and hating her rival, apprises the lovers of her father's design, and aids them, though unsuccessfully, to escape. When the guards enter to capture Ibrahim, Asteria fights in his defence, and is killed. The usual note of hatred toward her rival is lacking in this character. It is purely from unselfish motives and with realization of her hopeless love that she acts as she does. Charlot,[1] the girl disguised as a page who helps her lover win her rival, is another case in point.

The character of Thalestris, the Amazon Queen, stands out in sharp contrast to the conventional heroine. She is a vindicator of the rights of womankind and also the unsuccessful aspirant for Alexander's affection.

> "But I can never be his enemy,
> Nor can they others love who him once see."[2]

Haughty, uncompromising, not willing to partake his half love, —

> "In love and friendship it is too well known,
> They are but half friends who have more than one;
> And all who are true lovers like to me,
> Dread such a friend more than an enemy,"—[3]

in a moment of wine-exhilaration — on reflection, perhaps shocking, but not shockingly portrayed — she informs him of her passion.

[1] In the "English Princess."
[2] "Amazon Queen," Act 2, Sc. 2.
[3] *Ibid.* Act 2, Sc. 3.

"Though slavish women use not to bestow
Hearts on those men who do to others bow,
Yet thy great merit makes it destiny,
I cann't but do't, and in drink tell it thee.
Wine does make love like Spring-tides over-flow,
Else I should scorn you should this weakness know."[1]

She resigns herself with extraordinary complaisance to her fate, hoping

"Marr'age may help me yet with jealousie."[2]

She coolly prophesies that the marriage will be unhappy.

"Sir, your *Statira's* more than any she,
If she's without some hid deformity;
But if more knowledge should discover naught,
But that her mind and body's as it ought;
Yet all minds have an inequality,
Which will make them distrust or disagree.
For when *Statira* shall sometimes be dull,
Then love will seem not answer'd to the full;
And when you her frolick and wanton find,
Then you will doubt she may to more be kind."[3]

In a worldly-wise way she declines the invitation to the wedding.

"Excuse me, Sir, if I resolve to shun
The witnessing your being both undone,
But I have made some Amazons advance
To give your Majesty this night a dance.

[1] *Ibid.* Act 4, Sc. 5. [2] *Ibid.* [3] *Ibid.* Act 5, Sc. 3.

And I will wait i' th' morning when you rise
To see what charms remains in the Queen's eyes."[1]

Her story, disregarding the manner in which it is presented, is not unusual; but her opinions on the rights of woman and her championship of the unmarried state sound in advance of her time. She proclaims herself as

"The Queen of liberty,"[2]

and states her mission:

"This woman scorns some Husband's tyranny;
And all such female worthies we must free."[3]

Thalestris is a veritable Amazon, —

"By heaven she mocks me 'cause I had a slight.
Ah, that thou wert a rival who durst fight;"[4]

she tries to be thoroughly masculine:

"Though I, like men, have learn'd to fight and woe,
To be accomplish'd I must try drink too."[5]

Her discrediting marriage may be distinguished from the similar note in contemporary comedy,

[1] "Amazon Queen," Act 5, Sc. 7. This character is not to be confounded with the one of the same name in "Siege of Babylon."

[2] *Ibid.* Act 4, Sc. 5.

[3] *Ibid.* Act 2, Sc. 3.

[4] *Ibid.* Act 2, Sc. 7.

[5] *Ibid.* Act 4, Sc. 5.

where the end is satirical, or in the body of tragedy, where the exposition is made by a lover in defence of his disregarding the marital state. With her it is both a personal and an impersonal matter.

> "You use me ill to talk of marriage,
> I scorn to be your tame bird in a cage."[1]

She thinks of wedlock

> "As that which loseth womens sov'reignty."[2]

Her argument is more thoughtful than in the mass of similar passages in other plays.

> "For with a kind and sprightly liberty,
> They meet by natures choice whose Souls are free;
> Whilst marri'd fools, like Curs in couples ti'd,
> Would fain be running where they are deni'd,
> But each hates other as an enemy,
> For checking a more grateful sympathy;
> And so with dull and froward thoughts they get
> Babes like themselves, fit to submit and fret."[3]

The reasoning is more detailed:

> "I'l have no master for Companion.
> If I would take the air, I first must know
> If't be fair weather in my husband's brow;
> And all my dearest friends I must forswear,
> Lest he should think they are to me too dear;

[1] *Ibid.* Act 1, Sc. 4. [2] *Ibid.* Act 5, Sc. 4.
[3] *Ibid.* Act 2, Sc. 6.

My fortune too is his, and I must be
Stinted in point of generosity."[1]

Zelmura is the principal person in the "Siege of Memphis, or the Ambitious Queen."[2]

She is also an Amazon. Her fame as warrior precedes her appearance:

"the Queen did dauntless stand,
Terrour coucht in her eye, death in her hand;
The Heartless Crowd wondering, look up to spy
This new *Bellona* usher'd from the Sky."[3]

She wins the battle against the "Assyrians," and their leader Moarun. She offers to fight him single-handed, —

"For though a Woman I've a manly Soul."[4]

Honor prevents his accepting the challenge. His gallantry captivates her; so, when the king orders his death, she stops the guards who are about to take him away.

1 "Amazon Queen," Act 1, Sc. 4.

2 "This play is dedicated to the Truly Generous Henry Chivers, Esq., who shew' himself truly such in defending a play so full of Bombast and Fustian." — LANGBAINE, p. 183. "Zelmura, however, is a spirited character." — GENEST, i. 183.

3 "Siege of Memphis," Act 1, Sc. 1.

4 *Ibid.* Act 1, Sc. 2.

Still the king's admiration for her is unbounded.

> "Let other monarchs of their Subjects boast,
> I have a Theam will fill the mouth of fame
> His Trump resounding with a woman's name;
> A woman whose brave Spirit do's presage
> A happy fortune to Our latter Age,
> The Noble Carian Queen whose fame flys far
> For aiding Xerxes in the Persian war,
> She, whose renown through our East confine spreds
> For Godlike vertues, and heroick deeds,
> Would quit her fading claim did She live now,
> And place her Laurel on Zelmura's brow." [1]

Yet he would get Moarun out of the way. She not only intercedes in the prisoner's behalf, but commands the king to obey her wishes; and she speaks so strongly that his manner toward her changes.

> "Oh, damn'd Hypocrysie in woman kind." [2]

The queen straightway does act the hypocrite, feigning all compliance to her lord's will, but begs a boon which is no less than

> "The sole command o'er Egypt for three days." [3]

[1] *Ibid.* Act 1, Sc. 1. [2] *Ibid.* Act 2, Sc. 3.
[3] *Ibid.* Act 3, Sc. 3.

No sooner is this granted than she ascends the throne, has Moarun unbound, and the king himself, together with his son, seized. She next becomes aware of the mutual love of her sister Amasis and Moarun, and therefore prevents his departure, and threatens to stab Amasis unless she go to Moarun, and give him the impression that she no longer loves him. Amasis does this; but still, persisting in her love, the queen draws upon her and mortally wounds her. She attempts likewise to kill Moarun because he does not love her, and finally destroys herself. Ambition is the key-note to her character. She threatens to

> "Destroy the World, kill and disrobe
> Nature of her perfections, shake the Globe
> To its first Chaos, and by actions prove,
> Nothing can match a Woman's hate or love." [1]

There is much presumptuous daring.

> "And womens courage by ambition warm'd
> Dares laugh at danger, though all Hell stood arm'd." [2]

Her course of action is plainly marked.

> "Shall theams of Vertue make Zelmura pine,
> All ills of womans frailty I resign
> I bear a spirit brave and masculine,

[1] "Siege of Memphis," Act 2, Sc. 2. [2] *Ibid.* Act 3, Sc. 2.

My pleasures are my Gods, and passions birth,
Uncurb'd, and lawless is my Heaven or Earth." [1]

Zelmura is a "traiteresse," regicide, death-dealer to a husband, and a sororicide. Yet she was obviously intended for a heroine. Her audacity, doubtless, more than any other quality, won the criticism, "drawn with spirit." But the other characters in the play speak well of her. The king has already alluded to her "Godlike vertues and heroick deeds." Thus the sultan of Syria laments her departure:

"Farewell, thou type of never dying fame,
Whose lamp of honour shall forever flame;" [2]

and thus his son, Moarun, the hero, whose life she attempted:

"Injurious Gods, and too tyrannick fate,
That givest so noble lives so short a date,
That rob'st divine perfection of her store,
Which thus at wast consum'd makes Nations poor
Was't not enough, Oh, Envious, to subdue,
A Queen whose Second *Affrick* never knew,
But you must stop this Princess amber breath,
And proudly triumph in a Virgins death,
Heaven now, methinks, ungrateful do's appear,
These deeds had ne're be done, had I sat there." [3]

[1] *Ibid.* Act 4, Sc. 1. [2] *Ibid.* Act 5, Sc. 5. [3] *Ibid.*

Undoubtedly the explanation for this purging of her character may be found in the wondrous properties of heroic love.

> "Souls are not Damn'd if they have grace to Love,
> But blest with charms are fixt on Thrones above." [1]

In spite of these encomiums, however, which would place the Ambitious Queen among the heroines of this kind of drama, her character as shown in her sentiments and deeds is sufficiently like the woman villains of other plays to represent them. The incidents in which they are placed vary slightly, and according to these they have more or less chance to exercise their proclivities.

In general, such a character is actuated at first by ambition for power, and in the course of the play falls in love with the hero. There is usually no conflict between ambition and love; she simply resolves to attain both. Sometimes and in some cases love is preëminent, and sometimes ambition, and it is chiefly the stress on one of the two notes that distinguishes the characters from one another; and it is the absence of other notes (for jealousy

[1] "Siege of Memphis," Act 3, Sc. 1.

and revenge are but phases of the invariable disappointment, they are never drawn subtly or with distinction) that makes their common resemblances so palpable. Such characters are Laula, the Empress of Morocco, Kiosem in the "Conspiracy," Roxana in the "Siege of Babylon,"[1] Salome in "Herod and Mariamne," and Solome in "Herod the Great."

The characters arrange themselves then into a few groups. Their construction is so simple, so devoid of complexity, and they are all so enveloped and influenced by the spirit of heroic love that classification is not a mechanical matter of mutually exclusive types, but according to the emphasis attached to one elemental passion rather than another. For the fourteen characters, more or less, in every play, the list of "Persons Represented" itself not infrequently suggests and partly indicates their respective functions. In the first place, it is either stated or inferred that nearly every one of them is "in love with" another, so that "a lover" or "the lover" after a name would mean nothing; it would be a trite and useless comment. Therefore it is, doubtless, that the hero who is

[1] "Siege of Babylon." By Samuel Pordage. 1675.

none other than the principal lover is not characterized in the *dramatis personæ*, except possibly by the position of the name on the printed page. The villain is next in importance, and the fact that he is such is often boldly stated: Philampras,[1] a "Villain"; Ragalzan,[2] a "Villain"; Jasper,[3] a "Villain"; Bectas,[4] "a Rebel"; Smerdis,[5] "an Imposter," and Sulpitius,[6] "of a treacherous nature." On the other hand, Achilles[7] is "a great Champion of Greece"; Ulysses,[8] "a wise Counsellor"; Diomedes,[9] "a Valiant Confederate"; Sertorious,[10] "a brave Man, of a high Spirit"; and Mutius,[11] "a lover of War." Don Antonio[12] is typical of "a Jealous Lord." Of the women Alcinda[13] is "an Innocent Lady"; Perilla,[14] "a rich Widdow"; Andromache,[15] "the faithful Wife of Hector"; Cassandra,[16] "that prophesied the Destruction of Troy." The list usually concludes with mention of a "Friend" or two,

[1] "Marcelia." [2] "Conquest of China."
[3] "Fatal Jealousie." [4] "Conspiracy." [5] "Cambyses."
[6] "Vestal Virgin, or the Roman Ladies." By Sir Robert Howard. 1665. [7] "Destruction of Troy."
[8] *Ibid.* [9] *Ibid.* [10] "Vestal Virgin." [11] *Ibid.*
[12] "Fatal Jealousie." [13] "Conquest of China."
[14] "Marcelia." [15] "Destruction of Troy." [16] *Ibid.*

"confidants,"[1] or some such term, for the most unimportant figures.[2]

In the main these introductions are reliable and more than sufficient. They not only indicate but sometimes exhaust the character; description ends where it begins. The principal difference between heroes is not one of nature but of position, — of degree of importance. Major and minor lovers are the same in kind. Zungteus[3] is a hero of the first rank. Like him, on a minor plane, is Quitazo;[4] Muly Hamet[5] and Muly Labas[6] bear the same relation to each other.

There is somewhat more variation among the villains. They are actuated by a greater number of motives. Revenge for an insult prompts Cassander;[7] Ragalzan[8] thinks he should have been rewarded for his victories in war by the princess' hand, and was not; and Zachmi[9] would avenge a brother's death.

[1] "Confident and Creature," "Empress of Morocco," "Chief Servant and Creature," "Great Favourite."

[2] There is a "priest" when needed, but he is but master of supernatural ceremonies.

[3] "Conquest of China." [4] *Ibid.*

[5] "Empress of Morocco." [6] *Ibid.* [7] "Rival Kings."

[8] "Sacrifice." [9] "Siege of Memphis."

There are so few types that duplication and repetition in the same play[1] are necessary to complete the list. Thus it happens that the minor characters are for the most part pictures-in-little of the others; among them there is, however, a little more freedom of treatment than in the case of the major characters, and slightly more conformity with human nature. Holzhausen seems to think that in Dryden a minor character, *per se*, is truer to life. He says: "The weak Boabdelin and his faithless brother, Abdalla, in 'The Conquest of Granada,' likewise the emperor in 'Aureng-Zebe,' in a word those whose characters afford less opportunity for idealistic extravagance are conceived more realistically and drawn truer to nature than the high-flown heroes." [2]

There are a few plays having an heroic ele-

[1] As to the resemblance of the individuals of a given type in several plays, enough has already been said, although the oft-quoted extract from Martin Clifford's Letter on Dryden's borrowing from himself is ever pertinent. "Was not this huff-cap (Almanzor) once the Indian Emperor and at another time did he not call himself Maximine?" And "You are a strange, unconscionable thief, that art not content to steal from others, but dost rob thy poor wretched self too."

[2] Holzhausen, E. S., xv. 49.

ment that are distinguished by certain unusual characters not found in the mass. Such characters are in particular, Moriphanus in Mrs. Boothby's "Marcelia," described in "The Actor's Names" as "a proud, silly, rich fellow," and both the charlatan witch and the mad nurse in "Fatal Jealousie."

The scene of "Marcelia" is France, and yet Moriphanus is nothing other than the Frenchified fop of contemporary English comedy. The witch might be more appropriately treated under a study of the supernatural; while the Nurse, faintly echoing perhaps an original in "Romeo and Juliet," has, besides, a love affair of her own, and through it is led to murder, goes mad, and is killed by the villain. The rôle is mentioned in stage histories because it was played by Nokes with such success that he was ever afterwards called "Nurse Nokes."

The truth is, however, that these characters, and others like them, especially those of the comic sort, while not uncommon in other forms, are so entirely contrary to the heroic mode, that they may be dismissed from discussion. The plays in which they are found are hybrids. There is now and again an effort to lighten the too heroic tone of a piece.[1] But an heroic play with a slight admixture of comedy is different in kind from a comedy whose serious scenes are in rhyme;[2] and in the former this admixture is seldom introduced, seldom important, and seldom successful.[3]

After all, the effort to discover genuine individualization within the field proper is not well repaid. It does not appear to have been often attempted, and the attempt, when made, was simple and oratorical.

"*Antipater.* What is this, for whose sake you thought
My Father might from his Revenge be brought?
Since my Disgrace he did to favour climb.
Pholtiel. To draw him, Sir, at length, requires much time.
He is, to give his Character in short,
In War most fierce, most humble in the Court;

[1] "'Tis hard when a Man's own Wit runs so low, that he is forced to let in the tide of another Man's Counsel; 'tis as fatal and slavish as borrowing of money." — "Sacrifice," Act 2.

[2] Cf. "Comical Revenge."

[3] For instance, Ward (iii. 344) thus speaks of Orrery's "Altemira," "The author has here essayed a comic character called Filladen, but the scene in which he and the other lords review the ladies of the court is as devoid of wit as the lyrics interspersed are of charm."

Who merits favour, yet obtains it not,
In him unask'd an Advocate has got.
Respect for him he in all hearts has bred,
Because it is not sought, but merited.
Malice does fear such Virtue to pursue,
Which makes him favour'd without Envy too."[1]

The range of emotions is small.

"I know not what to do, I am so torn
By love and honour, jealousie and scorn!"[2]

This states the usual gamut. Since it is so, the tendency is for each character to become the exponent and champion of a single phase, a single idea, and the championship of any two phases on equal terms results in character balance.

The tendency is fostered by the liking for discussion for its own sake — a distinguishing trait of this drama. For instance, a faithless person is offset by an example of true friendship. Seleucus is the false friend; in the same play, Demetrius is the true. He speaks:

"I am resolv'd to do what I did vow;
For were I guilty of so mean a Thing,
As to be false both to my Friend and King

[1] "Herod the Great," Act 2.
[2] "Amazon Queen," Act 2, Sc. 3.

And should thereby my End in Love obtain,
The Joy would scarce be equal to my Pain.
Perhaps she will not be to me severe,
When sacred Friendship only made me err."[1]

And to "her" he explains:

"Yet to a Trust Fidelity is due;
That Man who can be faithless to his Friend
Tho' 'tis in Love, deserves to lose his End.

Could I but one unworthy action do,
I should by it forfeit my Right in you;
And tho' you might to pardon me think fit,
Yet to myself I ne'er could pardon it."[2]

Ptolemy[3] and Lysimachus are rivals and friends. The former cannot endure the rivalry, and desires a duel; the other declines to fight him on the score of friendship. They differ only in their attitude toward friendship.

Love and constancy are the only qualities which the hero and heroine expect to find in each other, and as the minor characters are but an embodiment of a single phase of the heroic idea, character development, as a feature, is not to be expected. There seems to have been no room for it in the scheme. Even passion, cu-

[1] "Tryphon," Act 3, Sc. 1. [2] *Ibid.* Act 4, Sc. 1.
[3] "Siege of Babylon."

mulative from act to act, till at last it seems as if all human words would fall short of adequate significance — which sometimes passes for character development — is not found; for there is frequently as much bombast in the first act as in the last, and thus a character literally exhausts his vocabulary, his greatest resource, early, and later he has outworn his old weapons, and cannot find new. The nearest resemblance to growth or any kind of alteration is in the case of repenting wrong-doers. Not all do repent. These either kill themselves or are killed in a characteristic manner, villanously cursing unto death.

There are, however, some repenting villains, whose remorse is either perfunctory — to satisfy the traditional exigencies of the plot — or more naturally, though still superficially, in the nature of character expression; their number is very small. The kings who desert their first mistress, unsuccessfully woo a second, and because of their failure return to the first, are obviously in the former class; the sultan in "Ibrahim," is of the latter. He is brought to a realization of his folly by the dying sultana relating to him the growth and decline of his love for her. Gradually, as she speaks, his affection returns; and she dies hearing and believing in his contrition.[1]

Although the characters belong to types, they do not represent humors. To say nothing of the comic, there is no suggestion either of physical or temperamental peculiarities to mark either individuals or groups. Dryden's use of the word "eccentric"—Almanzor a character of "eccentric virtue"—refers simply to a slight deviation from absolute perfection for the sake of human interest, such as "a confidence of himself almost approaching to an arrogance." There is no hint of a humor.

[1] The commentators on particular dramatists are agreed as to the absence of character development. To quote but three: Shadwell "neither knew how to develop character nor to depict its more subtle differences." — KENYON WEST. "The Laureates of England." 1895. "In Otway development of character . . . is little found." — OTWAY. Mermaid Series. Introduction by Hon. Roden Noel, p. xvi. "Morat's character ('Aureng-Zebe') is one of the few in Dryden's heroic plays in which dramatic development is not entirely lacking. On the contrary, there appears in him the purifying influence of love unusual in this kind. The stern man dies; the cause is not quite apparent; according to Hettner, it is of a broken heart (*l.c.* p. 91), after he has become reconciled with his faithful wife, Melisinda, and convinced of the vanity of his ambitious aspirations." — HOLZHAUSEN, E. S., xv. 43.

Such as it was, simple, not complex, rough, not fine, typical, not individualized, character was doubtless considered an important part of dramatic construction. There is every reason to suppose that the authors, each according to his light, so regarded it. Not only is there the direct assertion of their leaders, but the name in itself — heroic drama — implies necessarily the presence, and infers the importance of a hero. To portray him, as the term was understood in dramatic parlance at that time, must have been a primary object.

But how? The answer involves a definition of the heroic. Perhaps it might be claimed that as used here this adjective has nothing to do with the quality of the character, but only with its exalted rank, hence illustrious, hence heroic. But inasmuch as the model of the ancients is so frequently alluded to, it would seem that a contemporary interpretation would regard the great epic figures as in part originals.

It is plain that if this was the theory, practice did not bear it out. It is also plain that whatever the theory, practice did not bear it out. For the ideal lacked consistency. Here, according to Dryden, are the models of Almanzor:

"I must therefore avow, in the first place, from whence I took the character. The first image I had of him, was from the Achilles of Homer; the next from Tasso's Rinaldo (who was a copy of the former), and the third from the Artaban of Monsieur Calprenede."[1]

It was an interesting experiment, but was it possible for a character so conceived to be born in the world with a single spark of genuine vitality? There seems to have been a confusion in thought regarding the ancient heroes of Greece and Rome on the one hand, and the heroes of seventeenth-century French romance on the other. Now, the two appear incompatible. Dryden says that:

"An heroic play ought to be an imitation, in little, of an heroic poem; and consequently . . . love and valour ought to be the subject of it."[2]

But there was as little love in Achilles and Æneas as there is valour in the English heroic plays, not to mention the different meanings of the terms in the two instances. According to Dryden, Almanzor is the great-grandchild of Achilles, but the real kinship is no closer than if the intervening generations had been

[1] Dryden, "Essay on Heroic Plays." [2] *Ibid.*

indeed from the Homeric age to the fall of Granada.[1]

The English Restoration hero was the result of an attempt to make a composite portrait of ancient classical and modern romance heroes. The latter became predominant, and finally overshadowed the other, — granting even that the other had not from the beginning been blurred beyond recognition.

The incompatibility of the models had something to do with the result. But much more the heroic type was as it was because there

[1] Of course, Almanzor is nearer related to the heroes of French romance in general, and incidentally, though only partially, to Artaban in Calprenede's "Cleopatre" in particular. For instance, he goes over to the enemy when the king declines to release a prisoner at his request. Cf. H. Koerting, "Geschichte des Fransöschische Romans im XVII jahrhundert," 1891, i. 298.

Dryden's denial is interesting: "For my own part, I declare myself for Homer and Tasso, and am more in love with Achilles and Rinaldo than with Cyrus and Oroondates. I shall never subject my characters to the French standard, where love and honour are to be weighed by drachms and scruples." Holzhausen comments on this as follows: "At any rate, this last cannot be asserted of Almanzor, who, furthermore, was likely to, and actually did, give offence, in the age of Louis XIV and Charles II, on account of his contemptuous attitude to crowned heads." — HOLZHAUSEN, E. S., xv. 44.

is not any record of a single effort to produce an "image of human life" at first hand, and the failure is the more noticeable because Dryden himself applied the phrase to Almanzor. There is not a single instance of human nature being either the inspiration or the source of a heroic character. Knowledge of it was evidently not deemed either necessary or greatly desirable as prerequisite for dramatic writing. "Drawing all things as far above the ordinary proportion of the stage as that is beyond the common words and actions of human life" in Dryden's words must needs result, in ambitious as well as in inferior hands, disastrously: in the superhumanly extravagant, in general; and at the worst will so manifest itself as (to apply to a few a phrase that Genest uses for a single play) to "set burlesque at defiance."[1] There was a lack of restraint in the conception — "I

[1] The heroic drama is not without merit, but it was deficient in character delineation, and this deficiency has afforded amusement from its own time. "Without rant" — applied to certain characters by the critics — always signifies, comparatively, considerable praise, while some, such as Gray and Lowell, comment on the weaker points with great reluctance. Gray said enough harsh things about Dryden before he changed his attitude, but why Lowell declined to smile is not easy to ascertain.

love intemperance in all I do," says Caligula; an absence of poise, order, or anything that resembled responsibility. The desire for proportion is disappointed. In short, the Restoration hero and his train proved to be made of such perishable stuff because their composition was found wanting in that sense, which, to the exaltation of the populace they despised, is called common.

CHAPTER IV

SENTIMENT

I. *Love and Honor*

In the field of sentiment displayed by the heroic play the element of love is universal. Occasionally there is a character of importance not affected by it, as Cassander in the "Rival Kings." So few are such exceptions that love seems all-pervasive. The *dramatis personæ* of the "Rival Ladies" mentions no character without stating whom that character is "in love with." Other plays, in the course of action, reveal as much. This passion is not confined to human or mortal beings, but embraces unearthly spirits.[1] It is beyond human control.

> "We of ourselves can neither love nor hate.
> Heaven does reserve the power to guide our fate." [2]

[1] "Tyrannic Love."

[2] "Comical Revenge," Act 1, Sc. 4.

Its pains are foreordained.

"Ye gods, why are not hearts first paired above.
But some still interfere in other's love?
Ere each for each by certain marks are known,
You mould them up in haste, and drop them down;
And, while we seek what carelessly you sort,
You sit in state, and make our pains your sport." [1]

The hero is most zealous to declare his equality with or superiority to destiny in other concerns; but when love is the issue, he becomes a voluntary or involuntary victim. It is hard to exaggerate its importance.

"He who resigns his Love, tho' for his King,
Does, as he is a Lover, a low Thing;
But as a Subject, a high Crime does do,
Being at once, Subject and Rebel too;
For whilst to Regal Pow'r he does submit,
He casts off Love, a greater Pow'r than it." [2]

The passion is a noble frailty, and is so described in successive plays:

"Love is, at worst, a noble Frailty thought." [3]

"Loves the noblest Frailty of the Mind." [4]

[1] "Conquest of Granada," Pt. 2, Act 3, Sc. 3.

[2] "Henry V," Act 5. Added meaning is lent to this passage when Orrery's regard for royalty, as well as loyalty, and the divine right of kings is taken into consideration.

[3] "Black Prince," Act 3.

[4] "Indian Emperor," Act 2, Sc. 2.

"It is the noblest error of great Minds."[1]

Love is, in many cases, debasing.

"Hast thou been never base? did love ne'er bend
Thy frailer virtue, to betray thy friend?"[2]

"Witness, ye powers,
How much I suffered, and how long I strove
Against the assaults of this imperious love!
I represented to myself the shame
Of perjured faith, and violated fame;
Your great deserts, how ill they were repaid;
All arguments, in vain, I urged and weighed:
For mighty love, who prudence does despise,
For reason showed me Indamora's eyes.
What would you more? my crime I sadly view,
Acknowledge, am ashamed, and yet pursue."[3]

Wrong-doing at the dictate of love is justified;

"Blame not an act, which did from love proceed."[4]

But glorification and justification of love is, nevertheless, the usual attitude. The attitude is serious, but now and then there is a frivolous and sceptical note.

"Love is a Lye itself; there's no such passion:
And Truth to Women makes men most suspected,
Because 'tis rarely practic'd.
No woman takes herself to be a Monster;

[1] "Sacrifice," Act 2. [2] "Aureng-Zebe," Act 1, Sc. 1.
[3] *Ibid.* Act 2, Sc. 1.
[4] "Indian Emperor," Act 1, Sc. 2.

Yet she wou'd be so, if her Eyes were Stars,
Her Lips of Roses, and her Face of Lilies:
Why, Traps were made for foxes, Gins for Hares,
Limetwigs for Birds, and Lyes and Oaths for
women." [1]

Both serious and derogatory to love is the very exceptional remark of the hero of the "Siege of Memphis" on the death of his mistress.

"From henceforth drossy passions I'll remove,
And guard myself from the Curst baits of Love." [2]

Falling in love is seldom a gradual process, but usually the passion is born of and with the first glance, and in one case, at least, even before the lover has seen the object of his affection.

"In Athens late you nip'd my forward growth
And from my tender studies broke my youth;
Then call'd me to you from my Country far
To wait upon you, and to teach me War.
In Battailes toils, when you the day had spent,
You'd take me to you private in your tent;
There, as to shelter in some silent grove,
You'd shut me in, and tell me tales of Love.
Your charming tongue did ope my breath so wide,
Love shot in shafts, on which himself did ride:
When on Statira's Picture you wou'd look,
Faire Parisatis forme from you I tooke." [3]

[1] "Sacrifice," Act 2. [2] "Siege of Memphis," Act 5.
[3] "Rival Kings," Act 2.

Examples of instantaneous love are so numerous that it is commonly considered a characteristic mark of this kind of drama. The vastness of his feeling and the difficulty of a lover's fate are re-echoed.

> "Never was any lover's fate so hard." [1]

> "When men name one who lov'd to a Degree
> Ne'er known before, they'll say he lov'd like me." [2]

The effects of the passion are various; sometimes ennobling; as frequently, ignoble.

> "Ne'er more expect to see his Armour on,
> Perfumed and curl'd in Silks, he'll dance all day,
> All night his limbs on downy Quilts he'll lay,
> And sing his threats, and smile his frowns away.
> Whence is this change?
> Beauty, Sir; is the cause." [3]

Quite another strain and one oft repeated is

> "To lose her yet deserve her is more fit
> Then to posses her and not Merit it;" [4]

and,

> "That great Action I intend to do;
> If I her Right, above my love prefer,
> In that, by losing, I shall merit her.

[1] "Tryphon," Act 4. [2] "Henry V," Act 2.
[3] "Henry III," Act 2, Sc. 1.
[4] "Tryphon," Act 3.

And to obtain, not merit her, will prove
Less than to lose her, and deserve her Love.
'Tis worthy of my Flame, and of her Eyes,
To make Love be to Love a Sacrifice." [1]

The distinctive feature of heroic love is that it nullifies all other ideals in the lover, and makes him its absolute slave. Whether it be good or evil depends on the previous character of the man, though the lady concerned may often turn the balance.

There is some difference of sentiment in regard to the possibility and desirability of constancy.

"*Cleopatra.* Oh, tell me first, have you been e'er in love?
Hermione. Why, Madam, do you ask?
Cleopatra. Because I know,
That none can ease my Pain, that is not so.
Hermione. I was; but Love to Friendship did submit.
Cleopatra. Ah! 'twas not Love, if ought could conquer it.
You lov'd not well, or knew his pow'r but ill,
That say you are in Love, and are not still:
The Name of Love for love itself you took,
Since real Love can never be forsook.
Had yours been true, you might as well have swore
You do not live, as that you love no more." [2]

"But Love, when scorn'd, is justly held a fault." [3]

[1] "Henry V," Act 2. [2] "Tryphon," Act 3.
[3] "Black Prince," Act 3.

In action, too, there is variance. But in the entire range of the heroic drama, with hardly an exception, the principal lovers are constant to each other, and sometimes the expression of constancy is adequately worthy of the feeling. Thus Almanzor repulses Lyndaraxa:

> "Fair though you are
> As summer mornings, and your eyes more bright
> Than stars that twinkle in a winter's night;
> Though you have eloquence to warm and move
> Cold age and praying hermits, into love;
> Though Almahide with scorn rewards my care, —
> Yet, than to change, 'tis nobler to despair.
> My love's my soul; and that from fate is free;
> 'Tis that unchanged and deathless part of me." [1]

Among the minor characters, moreover, there is more final faithfulness in practice than in theory, if the instances of a man's returning to his first love be taken into account. In "Henry III," "Marcelia," and the "English Princess" a king deserts one mistress for another. In each case he returns. The cause assigned for this action in the last-named play is his doubting the virtue of the second mistress, and consequently going back to the first; but in all cases, as a matter of fact, he returns to the first

[1] "Conquest of Granada," Pt. 2, Act 3, Sc. 3.

without sincere renewal of affection, simply because he cannot win the second, and so, in compliance with dramatic tradition, there is nothing else left him to do. Thus a return to constancy may in itself mean nothing, but may even bear the mark of superficiality and insincerity.

Jealousy occupies a subordinate place in the heroic drama as a whole, for the reason that it is a characteristic of the inner being, and this drama deals primarily with the external. The lover is busy outrivalling his rival in ways most acceptable to the lady, or in physical combat against the enemy; and in the event of victory in either case, he believes marriage the reward, and he is not often in a position to question, or to have a right to question the attitude of the lady toward himself.

> "Examine jealousie and it will prove
> To be the careful tenderness of love.
> It can no sooner than Celestial fire
> Be either quench'd, or of itself expire." [1]

Chorus of Wives

1

"1. This cursed jealousie, what is't?
2. 'Tis Love that has lost itself in a Mist.

[1] "Siege of Rhodes," Pt. 2, Act 1.

3. 'Tis Love being frightened out of his wits.
4. 'Tis Love that has a fever got;
Love that is violently hot;
But troubled with cold and trembling fits.
'Tis yet a more unnatural evil:
Chorus. 'Tis the God of Love, 'tis the God of Love, possest with a devil.

2

1. 'Tis rich corrupted Wine of Love,
Which sharpest Vinegar does prove.
2. From all the sweet Flowers which might Honey make,
It does a deadly poyson bring.
3. Strange serpent which itself doth sting!
4. It never can sleep, and dreams still awake.
5. It stuffs up the Marriage-bed with thorns.
Chorus. It gores itself, it gores itself, with imagin'd horns." [1]

"He is with jealousie possest,
That Arrow, once withdrawn, must ever rove.
O weakness, sprung from mightiness of Love." [2]

Aureng-Zebe is an especially jealous lover, and some attention is given to the subject in the play.

"Small jealousies, 'tis true, inflame desire;
Too great, not fan, but quite blow out the fire." [3]

[1] "Siege of Rhodes," 4th Entry. [2] *Ibid.*
[3] "Aureng-Zebe," Act 4, Sc. 1.

Orrery's Tudor soliloquizes upon this passion in these lines:

"But, Fate, thou art unjust in making me
To quit the Love, yet keep the jealousy;
Which is of Love's fair tree the foulest Fruit,
A branch whose Nourishment offends the Root.
Shall Jealousy a Power o'er Judgment gain,
Tho' it does only in the Fancy reign?
With Knowledge thou art inconsistent still,
The Mind's foul Monster, whom Fair Truth does kill.
Thy Tyranny subverts e'en Nature's Laws;
For oft thou hast Effects without a cause;
And, which thy strength or weakness does detect,
Thou often hast a cause without Effect.
In all thou dost, thou ever dost amiss;
Seest what is not, or seest not that which is.
Whilst thou dost live, Sickness does thee pursue;
And he who cures thee, needs must kill thee too." [1]

Next to love, honor is commonly supposed to be the most considerable element in the heroic drama. The mere use of the term "heroic," with which love and honor are traditionally associated, is unquestionably responsible for this popular misconception. For honor is only speciously an important feature, as, notwithstanding the usual connotations with it of certain ideals, the heroic play was too late a growth to

[1] "Henry V," Act 4.

have the element of honor either of great extent or of vital nature.

The word is used in two senses: as synonymous with spiritual virtue, and as a course of human conduct prescribed by a code. As the latter, it impels a man to fight to defend a woman.

> "*Har. Jun.* Yet yield me Ysabinda, and be safe.
> *Tow.* I'll fight myself all scarlet over first;
> Were there no love, or no revenge,
> I could not now desist, in point of honour."[1]

Least of all may a man fight a woman, even though she be a warrior, and challenge him.

> "As thou art a woman I am Crost,
> And all the hopes of my revenge is lost:
> For to that Sex my honour makes me bend,
> Not fight against but with my blood defend."[2]

It regulates the etiquette of rivals.

> "Since we are rivals, honour does command
> We should not die but by each other's hand."[3]

It must be confessed, however, that "Honour's precepts,"[4] anything that implies the existence

[1] "Amboyna, or the Cruelties of the Dutch to the English Merchants." By John Dryden. 1673. Act 4, Sc. 3.

[2] "Siege of Memphis," Act 1, Sc. 2.

[3] "Conquest of Granada," Pt. 2, Act 4.

[4] "Aureng-Zebe," Act 2, Sc. 1.

of a code or "Rules of Honour,"[1] is but rarely spoken of, and never in a manner to attract, much less compel, attention.

In other words, the heroic drama, in the expression of sentiment, is not chivalrous. It is this that identifies it in spirit with the court for which it was written, and divorces it from kindred continental types. There is perhaps not more than a single mention of chivalry throughout its pages, and that is where Moarun refers to his sword as

"This brave badge of Chivalry."[2]

None of the heroes is vital enough, or in the true sense honorable enough, to reveal any of that fine essence of gentlemanhood by which the popular conception of chivalry is hallowed. As Courthope says, "Of the two great principles of Love and Honour, . . . one was now held to be non-existent, and the other was utterly perverted. . . . If ever there was a time when the instincts of chivalrous action (were) discouraged, it was in the reign of Charles II."[3] The

[1] "Herod the Great," Act 2.

[2] "Siege of Memphis," Act 1, Sc. 2.

[3] W. J. Courthope, "Addison," English Men of Letters Series, pp. 12, 13.

inspiration was too distant and the age was too unsympathetic for such an ideal. Honor is also used as synonymous with virtue, virtue meaning chastity in woman, and, in man, bravery in battle and loyalty to the state.

> "Honour is colder virtue set on fire."[1]

It is

> "A raging fit of virtue in the soul."[2]

This is the usual meaning of the word in the heroic play. But whether as a code or as virtue it is more often contemned than respected. Dryden's dispraise of the code was the result of reflection, not accidental, and is shown both in his critical and creative work. He says, "You see how little . . . great authors . . . esteem the point of honor, so much magnified by the French, and so ridiculously aped by us."[3]

> "The points of honour poets may produce;
> Trappings of life, for ornament not use:
> Honour which only does the name advance,
> Is the mere raving madness of romance."[4]

[1] "Siege of Rhodes," Pt. 1, 1st Entry.
[2] "Indian Emperor," Act 2, Sc. 2.
[3] Dryden, "Essay on Heroic Plays."
[4] "Aureng-Zebe," Act 2, Sc. 1.

But as virtue, also, honor is sneered at,[1] both by Dryden and other heroic dramatists.

> "Honour is but an itch in youthful blood,
> Of doing things extravagantly good.
> We call that virtue which is only heat
> That reigns in youth, till age finds out the cheat."[2]

> "If, when a crown and mistress are in place,
> Virtue intrudes with her lean holy face,
> Virtue's then mine and not I virtue's foe.
> Why does she come where she has nought to do?"[3]

Honor is not an ever present note in the heroic drama, but when it occurs it is usually placed in opposition to love, and almost invariably to its own disadvantage. Cortez' determination to follow love, when face to face with the two passions, is typical.

> "Honour, be gone! What art thou but a breath?
> I'll live proud of my infamy and shame,
> Graced with no triumph but a lover's name;"[4]

[1] For praise of honor, on the other hand, cf. "Aureng-Zebe," Act 5, Sc. 1; "Siege of Rhodes," 3d Entry; "Amazon Queen," Act 3, Sc. 1; "Don Carlos," Act 4, Sc. 1, and Orrery, *passim*.

[2] "Indian Queen," by Sir Robert Howard and John Dryden, 1665. Act 3, Sc. 1.

[3] "Conquest of Granada," Pt. 1, Act 2, Sc. 1.

[4] "Indian Emperor," Act 2, Sc. 2.

Yet those who disregard honor and give themselves up to love cannot escape a consciousness of baseness and seek to gloss it over by dwelling upon the "nobility" of the passion that enslaves them. The speech of Montezuma in the "Indian Emperor" represents the kind of sophistication by which the heroes endeavor to justify themselves:

> "Not that I fear the utmost fate can do
> Come I the event of doubtful war to know;
> * * * * * * *
> My motive from a nobler cause does spring.
> Love rules my heart, and is your monarch's king;
> I more desire to know Almeria's mind,
> Than all that heaven has for my state designed."[1]

There are occasionally exceptions to the general rule that love triumphs over honor and every other duty or passion. The "Indian Emperor" satisfactorily illustrates both rule and exception. In four of the characters of this play love and honor are conflicting motives. Three of the four succumb to love. The fourth, Guyomar, in the presence of his mistress, Alibech, declares his allegiance to honor. The lady, who holds the orthodox doctrine of

[1] "Indian Emperor," Act 2, Sc. 1.

heroic love, scorns a suitor who is not passion's slave, and promptly gives him his dismissal:

"*Guy.* What I have heard I blush to hear: and grieve,
Those words you spoke I must your words believe.
I to do this! I whom you once thought brave,
To sell my country and my king enslave?
All I have done by one foul act deface,
And yield my right to you by turning base?
What more could Odmar wish that I should do,
To lose your love than you persuade me to?
No, Madam, no, I never can commit
A deed so ill, nor can you suffer it:
'Tis but to try what virtue you can find
Lodged in my soul.

* * * * * * *

Alib. In all debates you plainly let me see
You love your virtue best, but Odmar me:
Go, your mistaken piety pursue." [1]

Although Almahide, in the "Conquest of Granada," like most heroines, remains true to her husband, yet love and the lover's position are exalted to that degree over everything else in the world that it is possible for Almanzor, representing the type, thus to address the husband of the woman he loves without detriment to his own heroic character:

"Your love and honour! mine are ruined worse:
Furies and hell! — What right have you to curse?

[1] *Ibid.* Act 4, Sc. 2.

> Dull husband as you are,
> What can your love, or what your honour be?
> I am her lover, and she's false to me."[1]

Heroic love is then the greatest element in the heroic play. It permeates the whole. It moulds other elements into itself, or sinks them into insignificance, and the few instances in which importance is attached to them may be considered either as a sign of individual originality, or at least as a departure from the customary sources of inspiration.

II. *Reason*

In the Epistle to the Reader prefixed to the "Destruction of Jerusalem"[2] the author says:

"But perhaps a man ought not to talk reason in love: I confess since love has got the sole possession of the stage, reason has had little to do there; that effeminate prince has softened and emasculated us the vassals of the stage. The reason why the off-spring of the moderns are such short-liv'd things, is because the Genii that beget 'em are so given to women; they court nothing but the ladies' favours, with them they waste all their strength, whenas the lusty an-

[1] "Conquest of Granada," Pt. 2, Act 4, Sc. 3.

[2] "Destruction of Jerusalem, by Titus Vespasian." In Two Parts. By John Crowne. 1677.

cients who fed on the wholesome diet of good sense, and used themselves to the strong manly exercises of reason have been the Fathers of vigorous issue, who have lived longer then the oldest Patriarchs, and are like to live as long as there are men. I, who am a friend both to love and good sense, endeavoured to reconcile 'em, and to bring reason into favour, not with hopes to rule; I desired only to procure him some little office in the stage, but I find it made an uproar, love would not endure such an innovation, it threatned his settled government; and reason is not at all popular; the ladies knew not what to make of his conversation, and the men generally sleep at it; that I see but little hopes of his preferment, which I am sorry for, since what future being I shall enjoy, I shall owe solely to him. Titus and Berenice as great gallants as they have been in France, and as good a shew as they have made in England, have not such a substantial fortune to maintain them for future ages, but I am afraid will be reduced to depend on Phraartes for a livelihood. The whinings of love, like a pretty new tune, please for a while, but are soon laid aside, and never thought of more; the same notes perhaps may help to compose another, but the old air is altered, and forever forgotten."

Championing reason's cause is, then, unusual.

"Oh! Why is Love call'd Nature's highest Law,
When Title, Man's Invention, does it awe?

But 'tis the Strength which reason does impart,
That makes my Blood give Rules thus to my Heart.
If Nature Reason on us did bestow,
Love, Nature's Dictate, 'twould not overthrow,
But Reason is a bright resistless Fire,
Which Heaven, not Nature does in us inspire.
It is not Nature's Child, but Nature's King,
And o'er Love's Height does us to Glory bring.
As Bodies are below, and Souls above,
So much should Reason be preferred to Love:
Since Glory is the Souls most proper Sphere,
It does but wander, when it moves not there."[1]

More commonly there is an exaltation of love over reason, and a consciousness of their incompatibility.

"*Abdal.* Reason was given to curb our headstrong will.
Zul. Reason but shows a weak physician's skill,
Gives nothing while the raging fit does last,
But stays to cure it, when the worst is past.
Reason's a staff for age, when nature's gone
But youth is strong enough to walk alone.[2]
Love ne'er was to Reason's Rules confined.[3]
To one in Love do not of Reason speak;
For Love is never strong, till Reason's weak."[4]

But according to some, Reason cures Love and succeeds it.

[1] "Henry V," Act 2.
[2] "Conquest of Granada," Pt. 1, Act 2, Sc. 1.
[3] "Black Prince," Act 3.
[4] "Tryphon," Act 5.

"Her coyness has made me her Sex abjure,
Where kindness is not, Reason is my cure,[1]
But Reason having now regain'd
That Throne where Passion lately reign'd;
Those Beauties which did charm,
Now may delight, but cannot harm." [2]

III. *Woman*

The heroic drama takes it for granted that reason plays a small part where woman is concerned.

"*Abner*. May it not, Sir, provoke her to despair,
Seeing another in that Glory share?
Herod. Perhaps it may — perhaps too — it may not,
Few women are by Reason lost or got." [3]

Man's superiority in other respects also is taken for granted. The following is more than the expression of an individual:

"I've thought his sister worthy of my love,
And shall descend t'accept her as my bride,
If I'm petition'd for't on every side." [4]

There is little verbal evidence of regard for female virtue.

"Madam, I go; but go so charm'd from hence,
Both by your Eyes and vertues influence,

[1] "Altemira," Act 2. [2] *Ibid.*
[3] "Herod the Great," Act 1. [4] "Charles VIII," Act. 1.

That 'tis impossible for me to know
To which I most of Adoration owe."[1]

But the more usual thought, prominent in Dryden, is the denunciation of virtue, particularly of virtuous marriage, because of its interference with love.

"In vain of pompous chastity y' are proud;
Virtue's adultery of the tongue, when loud,
I, with less pain, a prostitute could bear,
Than the shrill sound of — *Virtue! Virtue!* hear.
In unchaste wives
There's yet a kind of recompensing ease;
Vice keeps them humble, gives them care to please;
But against clamorous virtue what defense?
It stops our mouths and gives your noise pretense."[2]

"Love scorns all ties but those that are his own.
Chains that are dragged must needs uneasy prove
For there's a godlike liberty in love."[3]

"Love is a god, and like a god should be
Inconstant with unbounded liberty,
Rove as he list —"[4]

"Marriage, thou curse of love and snare of life,
That first debased a mistress to a wife!"[5]

[1] "Henry V," Act 3.
[2] "Aureng-Zebe," Act 2, Sc. 1.
[3] *Ibid.* [4] "Don Carlos," Act 3, Sc. 1.
[5] "Conquest of Granada," Pt. 2, Act 3, Sc. 1.

It is but one step to the curse of the sex, although there are not many such curses.

> "Ah! Traitress! Ah, Ingrate! Ah, faithless mind!
> Ah, sex, invented first to damn mankind!
> Nature took care to dress you up for sin;
> Adorned without; unfinished left, within.
> Hence by no judgment you your loves direct;
> Talk much, ne'er think, and still the wrong affect.
> So much self love in your composure's mixed,
> That love to others still remains unfixed;
> Greatness, and noise, and show, are your delight."[1]

In spite of the exaltation of love, there is not much laudation of womankind in the abstract; such laudation is rather of individuals.

These plays are not "problem plays." There is but one suggestion of a nineteenth-century remonstrance.

> "*Sebast.* But hold, I wrong Eugenia, if I blame
> Her, and not you alone, for all her shame.
> You rob'd her of her Chastity by force,
> Though fear of shame still kept her from remorse.
> *Fran.* Pish! Force! That was her policy to you,
> She did no more than what all Women do,
> Seem to resist what they do most desire.
> To raise the flame, yet seem to cool the fire;
> Believe this Truth, Sebastian, Women can
> Resist it, and perform it more than man.

[1] "Aureng-Zebe," Act 4, Sc. 1.

Sebast. Thus like the Devils we at first betray
Their Innocence, then blame on them we lay;
As if their guilt could have another cause
Than that which it from our Temptation draws."[1]

Though woman's rôle be a leading one, and love, her proverbial domain, the eternal theme, analysis of this passion and analysis of her character are lacking. The impression of blankness on the mind is caused not positively, but rather negatively, by what is not said. What is affirmed of her is for the most part conventional; man's superiority, woman's unreasonableness, dispraise of marriage, though virtue is oftener avoided than discussed. There is no ideal of womanhood at all at issue; children are not introduced, nor is there mention of any kind of domestic life; nor is there differentiation between woman and man in occupation or morals. She is neither better nor worse than he; there is no deceit, treachery, murder, or any manner of crime in which she may not partake. Love and war are the only spheres of action; in the first she ever is, and amazons, professional or amateur, are common.

[1] "Fatal Jealousie," Act 3.

IV. *Friendship*

In the strife between love and honor, honor as a dramatic motive frequently takes the place of or is synonymous with friendship. Hence the relation between love and friendship is identical with that between love and honor. As a sentiment friendship exhibits greater variety than love, inasmuch as there are no shades of gradation, no degrees in heroic love; one lover does not differ from another in zeal, but each loves to the utmost, as no one, according to himself, had ever done before.

Love is unconnected with any other passion, while friendship is often allied with the sense of duty toward a sovereign, and always, except in one important instance, it is intimately and paradoxically associated with rivalry in love. In degree, moreover, it varies from the mutual formal regard of courtiers, through the relation between confidant and master or mistress, of subject to emperor, of companionship among equals, to an intense affectionate devotion.

Owen Tudor, an Englishman in the train of Henry V, is at the beginning of the play a rejected suitor of Princess Katharine of France. That, in itself, would not make him despair, but the king loves the same lady and became enamored of her in the first place through his subject's description. In ignorance of Tudor's passion the king requests him to go to Katharine as a messenger of love from himself,

> "That my Friend should let my Princess know
> My flames are such as martyr'd Saints sustain."[1]

Owen does this. Afterwards he becomes so melancholy that the king, for friendship's sake, desires to know the source of his grief, and on much petitioning is told. Whereupon he resolves to do as much for Tudor as has been done for himself, which is no less than to plead his rival's cause before the princess.

This situation is an adequate illustration of the indissoluble connection between friendship and loyalty to a king. The same relation exists in other plays, but this is its most striking instance. The two sentiments are mixed; they are associated together, but the spiritual superiority of the former over the latter is insisted upon. The mutual faithfulness of the men

[1] "Henry V," Act 2.

is prominent; rivalry is the channel of the expression of this devotion which shows itself in their fairness toward each other, and, is augmented on Tudor's part by a sense of justice in resolving upon his self-sacrificing course through realization of his monarch's greater worth as a man.

There is a conception of the use of friends,

"For Ease of Sorrow, Friends from Heav'n were sent";

and abstract meditation on the subject of friendship, as of the other elemental passions, is a feature of most concrete instances, where the type is embodied. There are certain plays, themselves conspicuously heroic, which contain an element of friendship noticeable in itself. Some of these instances are remarkable, and for this reason a consideration of friendship as a phase of heroic sentiment is assured. Nevertheless, it is its prominence in individual plays rather than its presence in the body at large that entitles it to consideration. For it is not in all the plays but is confined to the compositions of a few men. Pordage and Bankes are among them, and in Orrery it is so much in evidence as to leave the impression of an individual characteristic. The constant repetition in his work of situations, the subject of which is friendship, is very noticeable, and is plainly a defect.

The fact that friendship as a prominent element of dramatic interest is confined to a few plays, in contrast to the mass of heroic sentiment which is peculiar to no one, two, or three writers, but was of universal use, suggests originality, and in the narrow sense of implying a distinguishing trait between Orrery and his dramatic contemporaries the suggestion is valid enough. But a plea for originality applied to any phase of the English heroic drama must needs be made cautiously.

V. *The People*

The following extracts indicate how thoroughly anti-democratic the sentiment of the heroic drama is. Oroondates and his confidant, on mention of the ambassadors, express themselves as to the common people in this manner:

"*Ara.* 'Twere fit you talk'd of something that procures
A grateful peace with your Ambassadors.

Oroo. These are the furies of the people's Brain,
That dare to sit upon a monarch's raign;
Not all the fire, nor all the fiends of Hell
Can act the rage that in Plebeians dwell;
When they are mad and know not what 'tis for,
Like winds they bustle, and like waves they roar;
On those above 'em look with Envies stings,
And mad because they cannot all be Kings.
Ara. At Kings they let their gorged stomachs fly,
Belching out treason, sprung from Luxury,
Behold with censures still bright Majesty;
As base astronomers look up and pray
Into the glorious Planets of the sky.
Oroo. Mercy the curse of Monarchs in this age,
That breeds this plague, that shou'd be quell'd by rage;
I'le like a Lion shake my angry locks
And fright the Souls out of this Coward Herd,
And make them put their Necks into their Yoaks —
Amb. Great Prince —
Oroo. Begone — You shall have your reward,
You thought me dead, or els from pow'r debar'd; —
I'le send you home with Chaines upon your feet,
With that reward you shall your Masters greet.
[*Exeunt* AMB. *bowing.*"[1]

The old emperor in "Aureng-Zebe" calls

"The vulgar, a scarce animated clod,
Ne'er pleased with aught above them, prince or God."[2]

And the hero says,

"The people's love so little I esteem."[3]

[1] "Rival Kings," Act 4.
[2] "Aureng-Zebe," Act 3, Sc. 1. [3] *Ibid.*

Such are some of the statements. As a matter of fact, verbal anti-democratic expressions are not numerous, but that there are none contradictory in sentiment to the above strengthens the case. It may be recalled that Shakespeare repeatedly puts into the mouths of many characters words equally derogatory to the merit of everyday citizens, the difference being that in him the citizen's cause is championed, even though unfairly, both by the presence of citizens upon the stage, and also their utterance of certain sentiments that are sufficient at least to arouse discussion. In other words the people are discussed, if not impartially championed, in Shakespeare. But in the heroic drama there is no such discussion. There is no appearance of a representative of the people, and they themselves are as a rule completely left out of consideration.

VI. *Patriotism*

Patriotism is shown in the heroic play either by the author laying the scene of his literary labors in his own country, or, less superficially, in the repetition of the virtues of Englishmen.

There are four English plays with English

scene and theme.[1] In them, if anywhere, presupposition of the presence of the patriotic note is most natural. "Edgar, or The English Monarch" augurs well for a title. But here is nothing English except the names, although the Advertisement has it that "The Histories examined, nothing in the Fable can seem Romantick or affected. But I must appeal from the late Epitomizers, who make Edgar point-blank guilty of Ethelwold's Death, without any sufficient ground from Antiquity."

To the modern reader the fable does seem affected; the characters influence it, and it is expressly stated as to Edgar that

> "Unking'd, in Love, we represent him here." [2]

His kingship is not concerned. He is a lover, the lover, nor more nor less. In the play itself there is not even a shadow of a patriotic sentiment. In the prologue to a tragedy three years earlier than "Edgar" is this auspicious announcement:

> "To plain Hollinshead and downright Stow
> We the coarse web of our Contrivance owe.

[1] "Black Prince," "Edgar," "English Princess," "Boadicea."

[2] "Edgar." Address to the King.

Greece, the first Mistress of the Tragic Muse,
To grace her Stage did her own Heroes chuse;
Their pens adorn'd their Native Swords; and thus
What was not Grecian past for Barbarous.
On us our Country the same duty lays,
And English Wit should English Valour raise.
Why should our Land to any Land submit
In choice of heroes, or in height of wit?
This made him write, who never writ till now,
Only to show what better pens should do.
And for his pains he hopes he shall be thought
(Though a bad Poet) a good Patriot." [1]

Disappointment follows — truly not in the expectation of "bad poetry," which is realized perfectly. The play is English, in the sense that "The Persons," as the cast is called, bear historical names, in some mention of events and places, and in preserving the outline of the popular story of the latter years and death of Richard III, but laudation of country or countrymen is too slight to notice.

The author's implication that he was doing something new in treating British history does not seem to have been strictly just to one of his illustrious contemporaries, for the "History of Henry V," written in rhyme, was acted in

[1] "English Princess."

1664, and in it, inconsiderable as praise of countrymen and countrywomen is, there is more than in the "English Princess."

"But Fame can want no Theme, when she does sing
Of *English* Swords led by an *English* King"

"*England* still affords
Beauties resistless as the *English* Swords."[1]

The French Queen chides her counsellor for esteeming their foes too highly, but he answers

"Ourselves we best excuse in praising them."[2]

But Caryl's inference was probably true in a more narrowly literal sense, as the scene of "Henry V" is laid in France, and it is moreover a "History," while the only "Heroic Tragedy" treating an English theme, with scene in England, that would have a claim to priority, is the "Black Prince," also by Orrery, which was produced six months after the "English Princess."[3]

One play has no more patriotism than the other, in spite of their prologues. That of the "Black Prince" is "Spoken by the Genius

[1] "Henry V," Act 1. [2] *Ibid.*

[3] The obvious but inconsequential comparison between Caryl and Shakespeare in this single respect was made by Warburton and amplified by Genest. Cf. Genest, i. 74.

of England, holding a Trident in one Hand, and a Sword in the other."

"Is England's Genius, that victorous name,
Which shakes the World, and fills the mouth of Fame,
So much forgot, as you misspend your Wit
(Which my great Deeds as gentle might have writ)
To court a Fancy, or improve a Dream,
And seek new Worlds for a less noble theme?
Can you in arms conspiring Nations see,
And think on anything but Fame and me?

* * * * * * *

This Sword, which in French blood so often dy'd,
Intail'd Success on the young Edward's Side,
Resigned to you, shall all those Arts exceed,
Which made him triumph, and that Kingdom bleed.
Their frighted lilies shall confess their Loss,
Wearing the crimson Liv'ry of your Cross;
And all the World shall learn by their Defeat,
Our Charles, not theirs, deserves the name of Great."

Thus among the earliest of the rhymed tragedies there were two as native in subject as their manner was foreign — the manner became fashionable, and dozens of plays were so written, but native matter was of infrequent recurrence. There was, besides, "Boadicea, Queen of Britain."[1] But in this play the patriotic note, which consists of lauding the bravery of the

[1] "Boadicea, Queen of Britain." By Charles Hopkins. 1697.

natives, is neither prominent nor otherwise remarkable.

The single play in which Dryden had a legitimate right to express patriotism was "Amboyna," a political pamphlet in dramatic form, where his loyalty to country as opposed to political loyalty is shown by making the Englishmen in the play models of all that is virtuous — the more sharply to contrast them with the perfidious Dutch — and by seldom inserted lines, such as

> "Wounds but awaken English courage." [1]

The dramas with English scene reveal no patriotism in content; the story of a British king's conquest of the French country and princess contains very little more. In "Henry III," however, where all the characters, the scene, and theme are French, the English patriotism of the author is more in evidence than in all the other plays combined.

> "His scenes, such as they are, in France are laid;
> Where you may see the ancient English Trade,
> Either in beating France or giving aid.
> Such vertue reign'd then in our smiles or frowns,
> Those did defend, as these could conquer crowns.

[1] "Amboyna," Act 4, Sc. 3.

These Miracles were in Eliza's reign
Whose left hand France and Holland did sustain,
And whose right hand both baffled Rome and Spain.
Whilst England only could the World subdue;
Nay, found a new one out, and reign'd there too;
Judge then what now Great Brittany may do!
Since now her helm a greater Prince does guide
Who has th' advantage of his Sex beside.
Tho here our poet rather would make known
His country's reputation than his own."[1]

Two Frenchmen are speaking of English prowess and of Elizabeth.

"*Car.* Yet Heav'n reveng'd our wrongs; as witness bear
The English Lions; who so oft did tear
Our lilies from their stems; and did advance
Their ensigns on our walls, and conquer'd France.
Guise. Look but how judgment prosecutes them still!
What England once has done, again she will.
That British harpy, who robs all the gain,
And watches o'er the golden Mines of Spain;
Whose Canvas wings about the World have flown,
As by that charm she'd circle in her own.
A Virgin! Who her neighb'ring Kings outbraves,
Scorning to match with her intended slaves.
This Heretick, this Woman, dares combine
Against our League, and with Navar does join."[2]

The bravery of the English and their queen is dwelt on.

[1] "Henry III." Prologue.
[2] *Ibid.* Act 1, Sc. 1.

"*Cap.* Th' English (valianter perchance than wise)
Bravely defi'd 'em scorning a surprise.
But a *Defiance* that their rage became;
Whose words were Bullets, and whose breath was flame.

* * * * * * *

King. The brav'ry of these *English* are so great
It is no shame that us so oft they beat.

* * * * * * *

Nav. That British Heroine, without controul,
Asserts the truth, no Sex is in the soul.
Valiant and wise as Pallas does appear;
A Goddess arm'd with beauty and a Spear.

* * * * * * *

Cap. France, Scotland, Ireland, Flanders, Holland boasts
The sev'ral Ships surpris'd upon their Coasts.
The British Lyons glutted, took their rests,
Vouchsafing offals to the lesser Beasts.
Nav. Thus in a word th' effects of seven years cost,
By English valor in seven days were lost.
King. The World shall never, nor has ever seen
A braver Nation or a braver Queen.
Her Neighbors justly may receive her Law.
Since she rules those who keep the World in awe."[1]

Joan of Orleans was learned in "Necromantick art," and therefore it was that her

"Powerful charms made the *English* quit the field;
No mortal force else could have made 'em yield."[2]

[1] *Ibid.* Act 4, Sc. 1.
[2] *Ibid.* Act 2, Sc. 2.

VII. *Summary*

This kind of drama is so permeated with the spirit of heroic love that other elements are always secondary, and investigation reveals only the extent of their comparative insignificance. The note of patriotism which might be expected from the mere titles of some of the plays, and which would strengthen the case of the native as opposed to the foreign constitution of the species, is the more noticeable wherever it is heard, because not general. The treatment of woman was inspired by a moribund literary tradition which could not give her the vitality either of sixteenth or of eighteenth century creations. The restriction of all characters to a single social class — that of illustrious birth — shows how exceedingly narrow the sphere of the heroic play was in its sympathies, and consequently how few the ideas must be, and what a limited compass they had to range in. Love and honor were the only themes, and by honor was meant all that was not love, and no matter under what name this went, whether war, ambition, reason, or friendship, it was considered as a form of honor;

its mission was only to act as a foil for the display of love; and only in this comprehensive sense of honor representing all that was not love were love and honor the subjects of the heroic play. Love is invariable, permanent, and dominant. Honor is of varying importance. But under the name of friendship it reaches, especially in Orrery, its highest and most influential form. There the strife between it and love is a strife between equals, and honor is exalted. Usually, however, it loses the victory:

> "Honour to this exploit would me soon call,
> But that love's Magick does surmount it all." [1]

So a discussion of the sentiment of the heroic play in its various forms of attitude toward ambition, reason, friends, country, and countrymen must needs return to its starting-point — heroic love.

The prologues and epilogues to these plays are perhaps the most fertile mine of information in regard to them. They frequently suggest that the dramatists themselves were quite aware of what they were doing in depicting this passion, aware of its power, of its un-English origin, and of its recent importation:

[1] "Amazon Queen," Act 2, Sc. 2.

"How many has our Rhimer kill'd to day?
What need of Siege and Conquest in a Play,
When Love can do the work as well as they?
Yet 'tis such Love as you've scarce met before:
Such Love I'm sure as English ground ne'er bore."[1]

[1] "Ibrahim." Epilogue.

CHAPTER V

GENERAL TRAITS

THE English heroic drama has the greatest variety in its scene of action, its historical setting chronologically and geographically considered. In time it extends from the "state of innocence"[1] to a period contemporary with its own rise. It were doubtless safer to confine its space to the earth, in spite of the frequency of supernatural intervention, and of the confident assertion by certain of the characters as to their control over their own actions after death. The hero struts over five continents, with little method in his journeyings. He is in England, France, Italy, Hungary, with a preference always for the imperfectly known and more remote lands.

These plays may be classed with reference to their geography as Eastern or Oriental, and

[1] "State of Innocence and Fall of Man." By John Dryden. 1674.

Western or Occidental. The former group lays its scenes in Asia, Africa, and the Moorish and Ottoman parts of Europe; the latter, in classical and Christian Europe and America. Of the Eastern plays concerned with ancient subjects, "Antony and Cleopatra" and the "Siege of Memphis" are African; the others are Asiatic. Sometimes the scene is picturesquely indefinite, as "The Banks of the River Thermidon, on the Borders of the Amazon's Country," but usually it is indicated by a single word, Eden, Persia, Syria, with Jerusalem and Babylon as centres. The stories of this class cover a period from the beginning of things to the fall of Jerusalem. There is, moreover, a modern Eastern group that lays its scenes in the centuries between the period indicated by the title of Settle's play, the "Conquest of China by the Tartars," and a time contemporary with the author of the plays themselves. The scenes of the modern as of the ancient group, are, in the main, Asiatic. Persia is common ground for both groups. In the modern group the action is played out among other lands in China, the East Indies and India, Morocco, the Island of Rhodes,

Granada, Turkey, and the region where the Turks fought the Hungarians.

The classical plays with a well-known historical background are the "Destruction of Troy," "Caligula," and "Sophonisba,"[1] a story of the Carthaginian wars. Maximin in "Tyrannick Love" is the Roman Emperor. The scene of the "Vestal Virgin" is of course Roman. The greater number of the modern Western plays are historical, sometimes written with obvious, though secondary, didactic purpose. Such are for Spain, the "Great Favourite, or the Duke of Lerma"; in connection with Italy, "Charles VIII of France." Peru and Mexico are the scenes of the "Indian Queen," and Mexico of the "Indian Emperor."

There are several plays of French and English history, treated either separately or internationally. Such are "Henry III," the "Black Prince," "English Princess," "Edgar," "Marcelia." The historical element varies in its conspicuousness and definiteness. In the "English Princess" there is much the same cast as in Shakespeare's "Richard III"; the histor-

[1] "Sophonisba, or Hannibal's Overthrow." By Nathaniel Lee. 1676.

ical part in "Boadicea" and in "Edgar" is less familiar, and a little more vague; and in "Marcelia" there is only the statement that the scene is France and Sigismund is king. Most of the plays are serious. There are a few, however, in this group, in which the comedy element predominates. They are concerned with the present time, as is implied by the tone of "Marriage-a-la-Mode" and "Rival Ladies"; and is directly stated in "Comical Revenge." In the first and second the scene is Sicily; in the last named, because of freer, less conventional treatment, London.

The heroic element in a drama need not, and in fact not infrequently does not, dominate the whole composition; and consequently giving attention to it in some cases draws one to the border-land of comedy. But a pure heroic play was commonly styled tragedy, and tragedy avoided then, as had always been its wont, native contemporary subjects. If the scene were England, as it often was, it was of a past age; if the time were the present, as in "Aureng-Zebe," the scene was remote.

"But still the modest stage
Forbears to represent the present age.
Let forreign stories matter here supply,
Old Tales and known are best for Tragedy."[1]

Such was a seventeenth-century utterance of an established tradition; but in practice it was regarded only partially — to the extent of keeping away from contemporary Christian Europe for matter. The idea of depicting the life of the age in serious drama did not obtain as yet, and consequently known Europe was, in a manner, sacred. But there was no other region that might not become at any time the scene of a "dramatic poem." For, conventional as this drama is for the most part in plot, character, diction, and sentiment, there seems to have been an adventurous desire, on the part of its authors, to enter upon new lands untrodden by their predecessors. Dryden, by temperament so fearful of being radical, chooses as the subject of a tragedy a contemporary prince, though of a far-off country, and the first English play whose scene is laid in America, is, doubtless, the "Indian Queen" of Dryden and Howard, with its conscious epilogue,

[1] Edw. Ravencroft's Epilogue to the "Conspiracy."

"You have seen all that this old world can do.
We, therefore, try the fortune of the new."

The "Empress of Morocco" is another example. "This play, which for no other Merit, durst take Sanctuary here, throws itself at your Feet, as your Own; the Story of which, I owe to your Hands, and your honorable Embassy into Affrica."[1] While tragedy seldom dealt with contemporary subjects, and never unless the scene was remote, the domain of comedy was broader because of its traditional right to satirize its own land and age.

The heroic drama is historical in the sense that, with few exceptions, there is sufficient foundation in fact to determine the approximate time and place of action, — but often that is all. The name of the male protagonist, — Caligula, Richard III, Herod, — indicates as much. But the definiteness and completeness of this element vary in the entire body of plays as well as in that part dealing with French and English history exclusively. They vary in degree from such tales as that of Oroondates and

[1] Epistle Dedicatory to the Right Honourable Henry, Earl of Norwich and Earl-Marshall of England, etc., to the "Empress of Morocco."

Statira, and the Mexican stories, which are on the border-land of fiction and romance, to plays like "Henry III" and "Henry V," in which the audience must have been instructed, would they or no, so abundant are the historical allusions. Such plays and their like remind one that the stage even then, though less than with the Elizabethans, must have been regarded as a popular medium for historical instruction. To be sure, this instruction frequently and most naturally is associated with the inculcation of patriotism. Since the historical background is essentially so meaningless, the twistings of facts are not to be wondered at, complaint against them is trite, and anachronisms are without significance.

Notwithstanding the fact that many of the characters bear historical names, and their country is nominally mentioned, the absence of scenery, character delineation, or diction, whereby to connect any drama with the soil of its scene of action is well-nigh complete. The reason for this is not far to seek. The poet's aim was to paint a hero. And his conception of a hero was arrived at from the prevailing fashionable literary tradition of love and honor, and it was conceived without any regard to race whatsoever.

The neglect of racial traits possibly might pass without comment in a previous age. But it is pertinent to ask, although in vain, why that adventurous spirit which led dramatists in successful search of new regions, new races, was not accompanied by the investigating curiosity that should differentiate China, Mexico, Rome, one from another, and Chinese and Mexicans and Romans. There is no local color — nothing but nomenclature. Because of the "Ynca" one is supposed to be in Peru, because of the "wall" in China, and again, because of "The actors' Names,"

> "Fancy you have two hours in Turkey been."[1]

But even the actors' names are sometimes of no avail. In "Marcelia" the scene is France, and the characters, for aught said to the contrary, French; but their names are non-committal; Sigismund, Melinet, Lotharius, Euryalus, Almeric, Valasco, Lucidore, Peregrine, Moriphanus, Graculus, Du-Prette, Meraspas, Philampras, Marcelia, Desha, Calinda, Erisinia, Arcasia, Perilla.

[1] "Conspiracy." Epilogue.

There is a variety in character ranging from vagueness and superficiality, of which examples are common, to definiteness and the result of thought, such as Solyman in "Mustapha"; and from the purely fictitious and semi-mythological to historical personages presented, like Caligula, somewhat in biographical detail. But this is apart from the question concerning character delineation of racial traits. There is as little local color shown in the words and actions of the characters as there is of differentiation in the scene. Even such a bald statement as Perez',

> "I am a Spaniard, Sir; that implies honour,"[1]

is exceedingly rare. Zungteus is not Tartar, Achilles is not Greek; and the monarchs of the various kingdoms of the earth, so far as vital relation to their native lands is concerned, might exchange thrones without fear of detection or of comment.

The comedy of the period is notorious for impropriety of thought and language. The tragedy is the reverse of this. The prologues and epilogues to tragedies are sometimes in the comic manner, coarse and indecent; but they

[1] "Amboyna," Act 2, Sc. 1.

are extraneous to the play itself, in which the language is as far removed as may be from the improper. There is very little even of a broader sort of gallantry than is now the fashion, but which might be found then and later in the strictest society. Contemporary comedy abounded in questionable situations. In the tragedy a bedroom scene, in which any importance attaches to the fact, as such, is rare indeed.

There is one such instance in which the innocence of the characters concerned is finally proved,[1] and there is another in which ladies are rescued from the boisterous rudeness of soldiers.[2] In Dryden moreover — seldom else-

[1] "Black Prince," Act 4.

[2] *Enter* First Soldier.

" *Sold.* Two Ladies, Sir, are fall'n into our snare.
Capt. Dost think I came with women to make War?
Sold. When seen, you'l think it much the safer choice
To charge the strongest Regiment in Blois.
Capt. Are they so beautiful?
Sold. Gad! Captain, more
Than you, or all the World e'r saw before.
Capt. Go, bring 'em in. Sure they can do no harm.
[*Exit* SOLD.
I'm cold, and they may serve to make me warm.

Enter Second Soldier *with* Ladies.

Capt. Gad, beautiful! Fair Lady, I'm for you;
The other you may share betwixt you two.
[*They hand her.* ARM. *runs out.*

where — there are occasional scenes, in which the diction as well as the situation itself exhibits sensuousness verging on sensuality.[1]

In this body of plays there are not any adages

Arm. Heav'n lend me Wings!
1st Sold. There after thee I'l flye,
Rather than miss my Quarry. [*Exit.*
2d Sold. So will I. [*Exit.*
Capt. Come, madam, come. [*Hands* GABRIEL.
Gab. What do you mean to do?
Capt. I am in Love.
Gab. 'Tis now no time to woo.
Bless me! Your looks are strange.
Capt. I mean to prove
All ways, to quench my raging flames of Love.
[*Strives with her.*
Gab. I'l dye first.
Capt. How! Deny me such a bliss;
Which, when I have obtain'd, you cannot miss.
Gab. Not miss mine Honour?
Capt. No, 'tis very right,
No more than miss your shadow in the night.
I am resolv'd. [*Forces her out.*
Gab. Just Heav'n vouchsafe your aid
Unto a Virgin treacherously betray'd!
[*Cries loudly as she's drag'd forth.* *Exeunt.*

Enter NAVAR, *arm'd, with* Soldiers.

Nav. This way I heard the cry.
[*He pursues, after clashing Swords, brings in* GABRIEL."
— "Henry III," Act 2, Sc. 1.

[1] For example, "Aureng-Zebe," Act 4, Nourmahal's wooing of the hero.

and proverbs, but there is a goodly number of axioms and aphorisms. The play itself was supposed to be exalted above everyday life, with no intent of supplying the place of a manual of human conduct. The following are instances of such moral reflections :[1]

"He only is above Envy and Fate
Whose mind in sinking Fortunes keeps its height."[2]

"In Fears Men sin, I scorn to be involv'd,
What is it can resist a soul resolv'd?"[3]

"The valiant man is his own emperor."[4]

"I find
My timorous Flesh strives to infect my Mind."[5]

Where such reflections abound it is inevitable that they should sometimes break the confines of a line or couplet, and invade a scene. The result may be a discussion, as in the following instance, where the relative claims of expediency, under the name of reason, and of justice are in question:

[1] A selection from Dryden is given by Holzhausen, E. S., xvi. 219.

[2] "Great Favorite," Act 4, concluding couplet.

[3] "Herod the Great," Act 1.

[4] "Siege of Rhodes," 4th Entry.

[5] "Herod the Great," Act 1.

"*Charoloys.* Have you forgot that Vow, Sir, which you made
To th' *English* King, when France he did invade?
That Vow is to your Honour still a Debt.
Burgundy. A Statesman all but int'rest may forget,
And only ought in his own Strength to trust:
'Tis not a Statesman's Virtue to be just.
Charoloys. Those Words which lately you in Council said,
Have on my Breast a deep Impression made.
You urg'd that Acts of Justice are alone
What can preserve or must exalt a Throne.
Is your own Counsel by yourself despisd?
Burgundy. I then for others, not myself, advis'd.
Reason should still appoint us what to do.
Charoloys. You'll find that Reason has Religion too;
Which is by Interchange of Justice shown,
Doing to all what to yourself is done.
Blamount. You measure Reason with a crooked line.
Charoloys. High Reason to Religion does incline.
Burgundy. I, Son, Reason of Cloisters, not of State;
Pow'r seldom is religious to that Height.
Religion too, not Reason is, but Faith.
Charoloys. I fear, Sir, if such dang'rous Ways you chuse,
Instead of ruling both, you both will lose."[1]

The admission of debate into a scene sometimes leads to the didactic.

"Why was not Reason, by decree of Heaven,
To Man for his internal Monarch given?

[1] "Henry V," Act 3.

Our Passions over us the Conquest get,
And as They please, They cloud or govern it.
Love, Honour, and Revenge by turns bear sway,
And all Command what they should all obey."[1]

Certain passages, too, in which there is much historical allusion and patriotic eulogy, may be termed purposely instructive.[2] On the whole, however, this drama is neither preceptive or instructive in a didactic manner. Theoretically, the authors might claim that, as tragedy paints men better than they are, an attempt at instruction by example on their part is implied. Practically, it is questionable whether they thought much about it.

The heroic drama is serious; it deals with momentous events in a supposedly dignified and lofty manner, in a tone rarely broken. With it there is very little admixture of the less serious, because that would have been out of accord with the "French manner." There is, however, an occasional departure,[3] probably under the influence of the earlier English tradi-

[1] "Altemira," Act 1. Importance is added to this passage by its closing an act.

[2] "Henry III," *passim*.

[3] "Altemira," Act 2. A satire on woman. "Fatal Jealousie," *passim*. A satire on witchcraft.

tion. But in the main, it may be stated with tolerable security that wherever there is humor it is unconscious. There is sufficient humor to attract notice. That these plays were not taken as seriously as they were meant to be, the "Rehearsal"[1] abundantly shows, and there is good reason to believe that the way in which they were listened to partly explains Dryden's contempt for his audience, for there is no doubt that certain of his scenes were received flippantly, which he regarded as worthy of respect.

There is many a passage that at the present time appears ridiculous, and many a passage must have appeared ridiculous to contemporary auditors. There is no dearth of unconscious humor, though its extent may be difficult to determine, as in the following situation where a villain mistakes one woman for another and mortally poisons her. On learning his error, he apologizes.

[1] The "Rehearsal," by George Villiers, Duke of Buckingham, and others, 1671, is the most deservedly famous satire on the absurdities of Restoration tragedy. But there was a number of burlesques on particular plays; and the allusions to heroic plays, mainly derogatory, in prologues and epilogues and scattered profusely throughout comedy, are countless. See Appendix C.

"But your pardon I implore;
You're the first Princess I ere killed before.
Though murd'ring I have my profession made;
No Artist but may fail once in his Trade.
A damn'd dull, foolish —"

then as he turns to another character, —

"But Hang't let it die;
'Tis a mistake not worth your memory." [1]

There is no proof, except in certain infrequent and specific cases, that the idea of infusing an anti-tragedy element into his work ever came to a writer of tragedies. Many of these writers were ill suited for the task they set themselves; they were not born poets, but poetasters, who made tragedies in title and externals, but the times demanded plays, and the pattern of composition prescribed by fashion rendered imitation easy and counterfeit plausible. The time was ripe for the "Rehearsal" and its species.

In substance the heroic drama is a violent, distorted, and hollow echo of a dead ideal; in its nature it is not only removed from everyday life (which would perhaps not matter), but in its own peculiar sphere it is not adequately

[1] "Conquest of China," Act 4, Sc. 2.

tangible and does not make for conviction. This, in itself, exposes it to derision. The opportunity for parody is doubled when it is recalled that these rampantly extravagant notions were clothed in ill-chosen words and situations, due either to a lack of a redeeming common sense in the author or to his ignorance of his craft as rhymer or playwright.

It is only necessary to imagine rhymed tragedies acted at the present, and to consider their probable reception, in order to realize partially the difference in taste between an audience that would tolerate this kind of drama and our own, and also to realize, though still partially, the gulf between these plays and any audience whatsoever — how ineffectually they must have made their appeal. Picture the spirit of the melancholy Dane's father disappearing in this wise:

> "*Fryar.* Stay Spirit stay —
> — What's he who does behind remain?
> *Spir.* One of the Princes of *Lorrain.*
> *Guise.* Say, Spirit, must he wear the Crown?
> *Spirit.* That unknown Voice has knock't us down.
> [*The three* SPIRITS, *Rebel and Murder, descend.*" [1]

[1] "Henry III," Act 2, Sc. 2.

Not necessarily comical, but certainly devoid of the habitual dignity of its author is

"Now that the Ghosts are vanish'd I'll appear."
[*He makes a noise.*[1]

The actor whose lot it was to declaim this — particularly the concluding couplet — is to be pitied:

Enter a SOLDIER

"*Sold.* Upon the Hill 'twixt this and Orleans,
Right-hand the Road, I 'spy some Horse advance.
Capt. How many may they be?
Sold. Some three or four.
Capt. Why did you stir unless they had been more?
Sold. Methought they more and more began t' appear.
Capt. Some dreadful Troop of Thistles!
Sold. Gad! I swear,
I saw 'em move.
Capt. Some Troop of horn'd Beasts,
Or Trees with waving Plumes upon their Crests.
Dost think they were not Clouds.
Sold. I know not well;
I'l try once more and then may surely tell." [*Exit.*[2]

There is naught in the context to account for the presence of this line:

"Knock at your breast; may be you're not at home." [3]

[1] "Herod the Great," Act 1.
[2] "Henry III," Act 2, Sc. 1.
[3] *Ibid.*, Act 3, Sc. 1.

If Mr. Stephen's dictum to the effect that the element of humor in a play proves the existence of this sense in the playwright be applied inversely, the result in Dryden's case is disputable. His two chief editors differ on the subject. It is not surprising, therefore, that as his talent for comedy has been valued low, he should now and again be unintentionally humorous in a sort of writing where it was difficult to avoid it entirely. In him, as in other heroic dramatists, the ridiculous may be discerned chiefly in the ultra-extravagant, in diction, situation, and sentiment. Sometimes, moreover, incongruity between the language and the character argues an indifference to comic possibilities. Thus a wife who has had intrigues with a Dutchman and an Englishman, parts from her husband, as he is about to be led to death. She observes:

"Farewell, my dearest! I may have many husbands,
But never one like thee."[1]

The Restoration tragedy did not reflect contemporary life, materially or historically. There is apparently scarcely a single allusion to a

[1] "Amboyna," Act 5, Sc. 1.

passing event.[1] With a few political references, a few eulogies of the king, scoffings at Puritanism, and an occasional gibe at the expense of the court (which is not necessarily a spontaneous contemporary feature), the list is nearly exhausted, so far as material is afforded by the plays themselves. There was no attempt to invade the province of the comedy of the day, and depict manners. Incidentally Ravenscroft's opinion,

> "I think the business of our Nation
> Too sad a Theam to pass for Recreation," [2]

confirmed the practice. That tragedy did not depict the life of the time is not in itself censurable; but disregard of all facts, without offering adequate substitutes, takes away the sense of standing on firm ground, and is not at all compensated for by the feeling of having left the earth, without at the same time having been transported to a fairy world.

It is not a fairy world; but the characters in

[1] It is, of course, impossible now to determine precisely the extent of such allusions. They were made the most of by the audience. Pepys says that the "Great Favourite" was intended to upbraid the king for his mistresses.

[2] "Conspiracy." Epilogue.

large part are historical figures, and so should be accountable to human reason. Their general manner of expression is such as might be supposed to emanate from a "bad poet," and the situation which does not satisfy, the character which does not convince, the sentiment which does not please — all, beyond question, came from the same source. In short, the whole is artificial.

And it must be acknowledged that, as a whole, the heroic drama is monotonous. Monotony is one of the many consequences of lack of originality, none more conspicuous. The endeavor on the part of several men, similarly educated, to attain the same end in the same manner, makes repetition to a monotonous extent inevitable. The oft-told tale, told in the selfsame way, becomes a drone. Love is frequently defined with striking similarity, manifestations of friendship are duplicated, the same characters and situations are reproduced again and again. Because of this monotony, the appetite becomes dulled, and the clearness of the traits fades. For this reason, too, bombast eventually fails to attract attention. Some plays are without this element, but in the most of them it is a prominent and, at first, a striking feature. But the frequency of its recurrence takes away its force.

> "Let 'em redouble speed and courage too,
> Here like *Alcides* on the Phrygian sand,
> Rage in his eyes and thunder in his hand,
> I will attend what Fate so ill design'd,
> And death with Fame and matchless Honour find.
> My Courage shall surpass dull Natures bounds,
> I'l fright the insulting Cowards with my wounds,
> And when at last my life's a Prey to Fate,
> Upon their mangled heaps I'l die in State." [1]

Herod must have had a marvellous gaze.

> "Were your House reviv'd, did they all reign,
> My Looks would fright them into Ghosts again." [2]

The sun and the "king" of China share the universe between them:

> "The Mighty will from whence all pow'r does grow,
> . . . plac'd the Sun above, and me below." [3]

Such boasts attract notice at first, but they are mild in comparison with numberless others. Artificiality, monotony, and bombast are flaws in art; but bombast gets to be thought of as a

[1] "Siege of Memphis," Act 1, Sc. 2.
[2] "Herod the Great," Act 2.
[3] "Conquest of China," Act 2.

spiritual matter, because it is the customary medium for the expression of sacrilege. A pretty sure means of determining the type of the heroic character is by finding out whether or not the individual claims for himself equality with, or even superiority over, the gods. If the result is negative, he lacks a generally important, if not an essential, feature. As the disrespect is to the gods rather than to the Christian God, the shock to the modern is not so great; besides the absurd extravagance of the conception makes serious consideration of it nearly impossible. Yet, if seriousness be maintained, blasphemy is frequent as well as flagrant.

"I'm in Fate's place, and dictate her decrees."[1]

"Whilst I have pow'r, declare the gods, for me they must,
Or I will fling their Temples in the Dust,
O'rethrow their altars, all their Flammins flay,
And take from them, their Deities away.
Tell me no more of Gods, my pow'er shall be
My greatest, and my only Deitie."[2]

[1] "Aureng-Zebe," Act 4, Sc. 1. For further selections from Dryden on this theme, see Holzhausen, E. S., xv. 40 ff. Observe Dryden often violates his own dictate,

"Yet noisy bombast carefully avoid."

[2] "Siege of Babylon," Act 3.

"But what is death, or whither do I go?
To heaven, or some dark Region plac't below,
If any State or government serene,
Be where I am should hell encrease its spleen,
And strive to oppose, yet I would be their Queen."[1]

The Empress of Morocco has no fear of death and would seek to avoid future punishment through an ingenious stratagem.

"Hell! No, of that I scorn to be afraid;
I'll send such throngs to the Infernal Shade,
Betray, and Kill, and Damn to that Degree,
I'll crowd up Hell, till there's no Room for Me."[2]

Restoration drama, as a whole, was accused of being atheistic. Crowne thus pleads guilty:

"I have, in my *Jerusalems*, made too beautiful an image of an atheist; and atheism appears too reasonable and lovely. I am sorry there should be anything under my hand in defence of such a false, pernicious and detestable opinion. Some endeavour to clear me of the guilt, and would persuade the world they were written by a noble and excellent wit, the late E. of R——. But they were printed long before my Lord died his Lordship in his poem call'd the Sessions of Poets charges me not with theft, but my scenes with dulness and want of wit, and poetry, which he wou'd not have done

[1] "Siege of Memphis," Act 5, Sc. 5.
[2] "Empress of Morocco," Act 3, Sc. 1.

if they had been his own. But since there is too much atheism in those plays I am content they shou'd be thought not mine or not good. I had rather have no wit, no being, than employ any part of it against him that gave it."[1]

The charge of atheism, however, against the heroic drama, need not be taken into consideration. It is enough that the temptation to out-Herod Herod in bombastic rant is yielded to, is pursued to the utmost extreme, cannot reach beyond Deity, and so stops there. Besides, Jeremy Collier attacked the stage of this era — he was well equipped and plain-speaking — attacked it in all its phases of profanity, blasphemy, and atheism. He was so scrupulous as to object to "Gad" as an oath. Yet nowhere (though from his own point of view he might have done so justly) did he cite for condemnation or even mention an heroic play,[2] and what he saw fit to let alone there is no occasion now to disturb.

The heroic drama is very superficial as regards intellectual or emotional power. There

[1] "Caligula." To the Reader.

[2] Jeremy Collier, "Short View," etc. He takes exception to a sentiment of Dryden in the dedication to "Aureng-Zebe." Chapter II, pp. 166–167, 3d edition. 1698.

is not overmuch philosophy of life, and still less that is not commonplace. The necessity of love, of faith, and of courageous singleness of purpose in life is recognized.

"A shaken faith's the storme of tottering soules."[1]

"Faith is a force from which there's no defence."[2]

One should not fear.

"No, there is a necessity in fate,
Why still the brave bold man is fortunate;
He keeps his object ever full in sight,
And that assurance holds him fierce and right.
True, 'tis a narrow path that leads to bliss,
But right before there is no precipice:
Fear makes men look aside, and then their footing miss."[3]

"The minds of heroes their own measures are,
They stand exempted from the rules of war.
One loose, one sally of the hero's soul,
Does all the military art control;
While timorous wit goes round, or fords the shore,
He shoots the gulf, and is already o'er,
And when the enthusiastic fit is spent,
Looks back amazed at what he underwent."[4]

"Had life no love, none would for business live;
Yet still from love the largest part we give;

[1] "Great Favourite," Act 4, Sc. 1.
[2] "Tyrannic Love," Act 4, Sc. 1.
[3] "Conquest of Granada," Pt. 1, Act 4, Sc. 2.
[4] *Ibid.*, Pt. 2, Act 4, Sc. 2.

And must be forced, in empire's weary toil,
To live long wretched, to be pleased a while."[1]

Here there is no enthusiasm over love or life, the melancholy note has set in; and wherever the author — whoever he be — rests for a moment, doubtless utterly exhausted, from habitual rampancy of thought, the reflection is generally sad. At least, whether it be moderately or extravagantly expressed, meditation on life and its value is usually pessimistic.

"Life's a disease;"[2]

"Life was my curse, and given me sure in spight;"[3]

and likewise life is a cheat;

"By this we see that all the World's a cheat,
Where truths and falsehoods lye so intermixt
And are so like each other that 'tis hard
To find the difference."[4]

There is a more famous passage in the same vein.

"When I consider life, 'tis all a cheat;
Yet, fooled with hope, men favour the deceit;
Trust on, and think to-morrow will repay:

[1] *Ibid.*, Pt. 1, Act 5, Sc. 2.
[2] "Fatal Jealousie," Act 2.
[3] "Don Carlos," Act 5, Sc. 1.
[4] "Fatal Jealousie," Act 2.

To-morrow's falser than the former day;
Lies worse, and, while it says, we shall be blest
With some new joys, cuts off what we possest.
Strange cozenage! None would live past years again,
Yet all hope pleasure in what yet remain;
And, from the dregs of life, think to receive,
What the first sprightly running could not give.
I'm tired with waiting for this chemic gold,
Which fools us young, and beggars us when old."[1]

The rejoinder is hopeful, but the note is rare and perhaps not entirely convincing.

"'Tis not for nothing that we life pursue;
It pays our hopes with something still that's new:
Each day's a mistress, unenjoyed before;
Like travellers, we're pleased with seeing more.
Did you but know what joys your way attend,
You would not hurry to your journey's end."[2]

An old man speaks thus:

"Believe me, son, and needless trouble spare;
'Tis a base world, and is not worth our care:
The vulgar, a scarce animated clod,
Ne'er pleased with aught above them, prince or God.
Were I a god, the drunken globe should roll,
The little emmets with the human soul
Care for themselves, while at my ease I sat,
And second causes did the work of fate;
Or, if I would take care, that care should be
For wit that scorned the world, and lived like me."[3]

[1] "Aureng-Zebe," Act 4, Sc. 1.
[2] *Ibid.* [3] *Ibid.*

All is vanity.

"'Tis hard to know whose brains have wider flaws,
They who sit rattling chains, and plaiting straws,
Or they who toil only for vain renown,
To wear in history a paper crown.
Whilst Cæsar now for a design so vain
Takes poets and historians in his train,
How like a lunatic this Prince appears,
Pleas'd because bells jingling at his ears!"[1]

Old age is uninviting.

"The greatest object pity hath, is Age
When it returns to childishness again
* * * * * * *
And though we see this true, yet we would all
Prolong our time to that decrepid state."[2]

Since the world is a fraud, let us adapt ourselves to its ways, and believe not in immortal love.

"Think you then Madam, that no sympathy
Of noble souls lasts to eternity?

No, there are no such souls as you would have,
What ever you have read or heard that's brave.
Our Conquerour, whose force equals his will,
A *Hero* is, 'cause he can rob and kill.
And well bred Cheats, do call it complement,
When flattering they speak what is not meant;

[1] "Caligula," Act 3.
[2] "Fatal Jealousie," Act 5.

Cheating out-witting is, though some tame fools
Believe the virtue taught us in our Schools." [1]

Of course marriage but increases misery.

"There's not that happiness
In Marriage Beds, as single People guess,
No, no, so far from that, that thousands be
Flatter'd by hopes to endless misery.
And where there's two obtain their heart's desire,
Ten thousand miss it, and in grief expire.
Were these Positions true, there's no man, sure,
If Widdowed once, could other Wives endure.
And yet we see the first depriv'd of Life,
There's few that seek not for a second Wife.

'Tis true, though strange, but yet our minds are such,
As always find too little, or too much,
Desire's a Monster, whose extended Maw
Is never fill'd tho' it doth all things draw;
For we with envious Eyes do others see,
Who want our ills, and think they happy be,
Till we possessing what we wish'd before,
Find our ills doubl'd, and so wish for more." [2]

The attitude toward life is, then, pessimistic, its value is dubious; and the attitude toward things unseen is sceptical. This approaches the paradoxical, for there is a great deal of the visible appearance of the supernatural on the stage

[1] "Amazon Queen," Act 1, Sc. 1.
[2] "Fatal Jealousie," Act 1.

— ghosts, spirits, goblins, and the like — and in many cases there is no evidence to show that the scene was not meant to be serious, nor that it was interpreted otherwise. It would probably be difficult, in other words, to prove that such scenes were intended to be ridiculous; the manner is too dignified to warrant such an assumption. Furthermore, there are minutely detailed descriptions of charms, of means of appeal to the unearthly. Yet, the intellectual aspect, as expressed in verbal reflection on what is beyond nature, is sceptical.

"The Dead ne'er to the Living durst appear,
Ghosts are but shadows painted by our fear." [1]

Richard III speaks:

"Hah! Ghosts? there are no ghosts, nor ever were,
But in the Tales of Priests, or Womens Fear.
If you be Ghosts, to your dark Mansions go;
If you be Ghosts, 'twas I that made you so.
I of your Substance these pale Nothings made; [2]
How dare you then your Conquerour invade?
Go home, dark Vagabonds! must I not have
Rest in my Bed, nor you Rest in your grave?
What Magick can Night-Vapours thus condense
To Forms, which cheat, and terrifie the Sense?"

[1] "Herod the Great," Act 2.
[2] The punctuation is indistinct.

After thus addressing the apparition before him as if it did not exist, his mental state changes, and the address is continued, taking for granted the actuality of the vision.

> "Saint *Henry!* get thee hence to thy cold Bed,
> So tame, alive? so fierce, now thou art Dead?
> A holy King did not the Throne become,
> Thy Godliness prepar'd thee for a Tomb.
> I did from *Tewksbery* dispatch thy Heir,
> In the next World to be thy Harbinger;
> Would you have staid behind, when he was gone?
> A Father ought not to outlive his Son.
> Hah! Brother? Wife? stand off! no tyes of Blood
> Are by aspiring monarchs understood;
> They to secure my Crown did Life resign;
> She in a Cup, he in a Butt of Wine."

The scene and the act close in this way:

> "Peace, Conscience! I long since have conquer'd thee;
> Yet still thou art dispos'd to Mutinie
> Oft have I par'd thy Branches; but thy Root
> Does lye so deep, I cannot tear it out.
> Of Sovereign Power it is the only Curse,
> To be Successful, and then feel Remorse."[1]

The sceptical view is not confined to verbal expression; there are scenes also in which the supernatural is scoffed at. In the following, Statira mistakes a woman for a goddess,

[1] "English Princess," Act 4, Sc. 9.

and confides the vision to her lover, Alexander, who takes advantage of her credulity.

"Enter the AMAZON QUEEN alone from Hunting, disguised with a Head-piece, who is mistaken for Diana. Statira vail'd, prays to the supposed Diana."[1]

"*Stat.* Diana lately did to me appear,
And bid me love the man I held most dear,
And that I should not much prolong his pain;
But left the rest till we two met again.
So that I cannot be for marriage free,
Till the bright goddess next appears to me.
Alex. You are sure wrought on by confederates,
For we have but few parleys with the Fates;
But when the deities do ought reveal,
T'is to their Priests, what they from us conceal;
And you the goddess will behold no more,
Which fills me with despair more than before.

Stat. Sir, there were none who knew of my design
To pray to her when she on me did shine;
There was my woman, who me waits upon,
Who saw and knew 'twas no delusion.
Alex. But in what dress, did she to you appear?
Stat. A Head-piece on, and in her hand a Spear.
As fame does tell us, Dian oft was wont
So to be clad when she went forth to hunt.
Alex. 'Tis a good hint, an Oracle to fain [*Aside.*
From Ephesus, sought and return'd again."[2]

[1] "Amazon Queen," Act 2, Sc. 3.
[2] *Ibid.*, Act 4, Sc. 2.

Alexander therefore has a make-believe oracle presented to her, which she thinks genuine, and which she joyfully obeys :

> "'Twas honour and not I bred my delay,
> Goddess thou know'st how gladly I obey."[1]

There is still another play which is in effect a satire on witchcraft, or, more correctly, includes the story of a witch. Its authorship is doubtful, but the date, 1673, indicates that the play was written when witchcraft was a much discussed question, and the mere importance of the subject corroborates this indication. This suggests that it was in a manner more closely linked to its age than others of its kind. There were some famous accusations then for witchcraft, particularly one in France only the year previous.[2] Glanvil's book came out in 1681, and 1682 has been assigned as the last date when witches were hanged in England.[3] Considering the time, therefore, the modernity of the rationalism of the following speech is noticeable. In the same

[1] "Amazon Queen," Act 5, Sc. 2.

[2] Francis Hutchinson, "Historical Essay concerning Witchcraft," 1720, p. 55.

[3] *Ibid.*, p. 57.

play there is a scene in which the methods of witchcraft are exposed and ridiculed. In connection with opinions on the supernatural such as these, as well as on pessimism and scepticism in general, it should always be borne in mind that the audience as well as the playwright was of the court, which was a very different matter from being of the people. So, however prevalent in court circles, among comparatively educated men, such ideas may have been, they could not have been widely spread. The attempt to seek in this body of plays popular as opposed to courtly, expression of life and ideals, is discouraging.

"I've no such art
As People think, to call up Spirits to me;
Nor know I anything but what is told me.

* * * * * * *

These things you speak of, people think I do,
And so I'de have 'em, for 'tis the only way I have to live;
The Vulgar People love to be deluded;
And things the most unlikely they most dote on;
A strange Disease in Cattle, Hogs or Pigs,
Or any accident in Cheese or Butter;
Though't be but natural, or a Slut's fault,
Must straight be witchcraft! Oh, the Witch was here!
The Ears or Tail is burn'd, the Churn is burn'd;
And this to hurt the Witch, when all the while

They 're likest Witches that believe such Cures;

* * * * * * *

though I can raise no Devils,
Yet I confederate with Rogues and Taylors,
Things that can shape themselves like Elves,
And Goblins ——
And often do like Spirits haunt great Houses,
Most times to steal, but many times for mirth." [1]

Passages on death and immortality, as a final phase of doubt, are not as a rule noteworthy. It is the uncertainty of the nature of the undiscovered country that makes death fearful. It is difficult to banish Hamlet's soliloquy from the mind, and some passages indicate that Restoration dramatists did not do so.

"Could we live always, life were worth our cost;
But now we keep with care what must be lost.
Here we stand shivering on the bank, and cry,
When we should plunge into eternity.

One moment ends our pain;
And yet the shock of death we dare not stand,
By thought scarce measured, and too swift for sand;
'Tis but because the living death ne'er knew,
They fear to prove it as a thing that's new." [2]

"Distrust and darkness of a future state,
Make poor mankind so fearful of their fate.

[1] "Fatal Jealousie," Act 2.
[2] "Tyrannic Love," Act 5, Sc. 1.

Death, in itself, is nothing; but we fear
To be we know not what, we know not where."[1]

"What is the thing, call'd Death, we mortals shun?
Is't some real, or is't a fancy only?
Like that imaginary point in Mathematics;
Not to be found only in definition.
It is no more; Death, like your Children's Bug-
bears
Is fear'd by all, yet has no other Being
Than what weak fancy gives it; 'tis a line,
But yet imaginary, drawn betwixt
Time and that dreadful thing Eternity;
I, that's the thing, 'tis fear'd; for now I find it
Eternity which puzzles all the World,
To name the Inhabitants that People it;
Eternity, whose undiscovered Countrey
We Fools divide, before we come to see it;
Making one part contain all happiness,
The other misery, then unseen fight for 't.
Losing our certains for uncertainties;
All Sects pretending to a Right of choyce;
Yet none go willingly to take their part,
For they all doubt what they pretend to know,
And fear to mount, lest they should fall below."[2]

Although the heroic play is mainly non-reflective, dealing with externals, there is now and then a deeper note than usual, such as this on truth:

[1] "Aureng-Zebe," Act 4, Sc. 1.
[2] "Fatal Jealousie," Act 3.

> "So in Terrestrial things there is not one
> But takes its Form and Nature from our fancy;
> Not its own being, and is what we do think it."

Truth is not as it seems to men.

> "No, not at all, as truth appears to us;
> For oftentimes
> That is a truth to me that's false to you,
> So 'twould not be if it was truly true."[1]

Far rarer is the note that the real life is within.

> "I'm Pris'ner still, to my own thoughts enslav'd,
> There's no confinement like that of the mind;
> All other Bondage may releasements find."[2]

The heroic play is a strange mixture of a rigid adhesion to law and of utter disregard for it. In the main, law is observed in the various manifestations of external form, such as in versification and in plot. The purest examples of the heroic play are written entirely in couplets. Lowell pointed out that the heroic couplet is splendidly adapted for compositions of a mock-heroic nature, and that Pope's "Rape of the Lock" owes its perfection in part to his choice of this kind of verse. It is clear that a form

[1] "Fatal Jealousie," Act 2.
[2] "Henry III," Act 2, Sc. 1.

which lends itself so readily to mock-heroic purposes must be used, when applied to the heroic, with great discretion. But it was used in the reign of Charles II so indiscriminately as to obliterate in the minds of its devotees any sense of its appropriateness to the subject-matter. Perhaps it was this indiscriminate and excessive use of it that has strengthened the general opinion that the form itself is most ill suited for English dramatic expression. The words of M. Beljame, because of his nationality and of his intimate acquaintance with English literature of the seventeenth century, should carry great weight in this connection. He says: —

"They adopted rhyme. If this form seems necessary for the rhythm of our French verse, it imparts to the English a lyrical tone which is unbearable [*un chant lyrique insupportable*] in a work of great length, and it is so manifestly contrary to the dramatic genius of our neighbors that it was dethroned by Marlowe in the sixteenth century, and the Restoration poets could only give it an artificial life for a few years, after which it disappeared forever from the stage."[1]

[1] Alexandre Beljame, "Le Public et les Hommes de Lettres en Angleterre au dix-huitième Siècle." Deuxième édition, 1897, p. 41.

Many of the dramatists themselves despised the vehicle of expression which they used; Shadwell, from the first, Dryden, eventually, and the others silently. There may have been a few, like Rymer, who thought well of it; but it is worthy of note, in considering the men of more than average ability who wrote heroic plays and also plays which in form were not heroic, that it was in the latter kind that their efforts attained the greatest excellence. This is true of Otway, Crowne, Lee, and Dryden.

The plot, like the versification, was made by rule. The strict observance, on the whole, of the three unities, is in itself sufficient evidence of the wide application of the fixed standard. The method was not of the kind that creative genius imposes upon itself, but it was concerned with technique in the narrow sense, and disregarded the relation between internal and external form. In the characterization, the combination of features which adhere to a prescribed code and of others which disregard it, is noticeable. In so far as the *dramatis personæ* are affected by the exigencies of the regularity of the plot, they show they are made on a set plan; but as the mouth-pieces of certain sentiments which defy law and order, they reflect license.

It is in the sentiment of the heroic play that this license is most conspicuous. Here there is a most curious mixture of shadows of old ideals, and of old ideals perverted. There are some phases of heroic sentiment that undeniably, though faintly, echo and form a part of a literary tradition that the Troubadours began. There are other phases which are the result of the distortion of chivalric ideals. The note of patriotism is the most unquestionable and prominent native element in heroic sentiment. Not to be compared, perhaps, with the same note in Elizabethan drama, or even in the lyric contemporary with itself, this element is still respectable and genuine. It should be remembered, however, as a qualification, that patriotism never embraced the humble, never considered them individually but collectively, and then, even more than in Shakespeare's case, to abuse them. In the drawing of examples of friendship, the heroic drama keeps closest to the literary ideals of all ages; to the traditions of both classic and romantic poetry, and the great spirits from Homer to the author of Roland, to

Tasso, Ariosto, and the more modern poets. They have all exalted friendship; so it is in the heroic play. Virtue is often sneered at, reason and honor are brushed contemptuously aside; friendship alone has its place upon a high plane, second only in elevation to that upon which love is enthroned.

The contempt for honor was a conscious breaking away from the contemporary French standard and most clearly illustrates the inversion and subversion of a literary tradition. Heroic love is not a high and ennobling passion, but one which has this great and distinctive peculiarity that it sanctions a violation of all moral laws wherever they are opposed to its free sweep and range, although, when not conflicting with love, they are recognized as laws to which man owes allegiance, and ideals of conduct toward which he should work. The doctrine that love justifies wrong-doing is incompatible with poetic justice, which, consequently, is not always regarded. Yet love in this drama is still dignified and serious, with the physical element cast in the background, and constancy extolled.

The native element in the heroic play is

slight, for the love which is the most important feature of heroic sentiment and the three unities which determined the external form are foreign to England. The only claim to originality that plays with these predominating characteristics can have is based on the general truth that the importation of anything, from a country in which it is in accord with the national temperament, to another land the native genius of which is incapable of assimilating it, always results in something different from the original. In verse-form, plot, character, and sentiment, the heroic play was exotic. It was frankly introduced as a foreign thing to please a Frenchified court. Its failure was due first to its being antagonistic to the British dramatic genius and secondly to the fact that no other type of English drama appealed to an audience which was so restricted in taste and so small in numbers.

Artificial, monotonous, and bombastic as an art production; spiritually superficial, pessimistic, sceptical in its reflections on life, blasphemous and not overmuch observing of poetic justice, the heroic drama has for its sphere the external life of pomp and pageantry, essentially unideal. Yet, with all its faults, it was a wholesome antidote to the shameless affronts to taste and morals for which contemporary comedy is notorious. It insisted upon decency and decorum of language, it encouraged many of the virtues, such as generosity and bravery, and consistently kept aloof from the sordid cares of everyday life. To a public tainted with meanness and sensuality it presented a shadow, at least, of true heroic character.

APPENDIX A

RELATION BETWEEN THE HEROIC PLAY AND THE OPERA

Though the "Siege of Rhodes" is usually termed the first English opera, particularly by writers of literary histories, the resemblance of opera form to the masque is plain, and has been pointed out. "The idea of English Opera was suggested neither by the Ballet nor the Tragedy. It was the legitimate offspring of the Masque; and the Masque, in England at least, was very far from presenting the characteristics of a true Lyric Drama. Its music was, at first, purely incidental — as much so as that introduced into the plays of Shakespeare. . . . The music written by Henry Lawes for Milton's 'Comus' in 1634 is far less dramatic than Lock's 'Macbeth'; and it was really Purcell who first transformed the Masque into the opera; or rather, annihilated the one, and introduced the other in its place." — GROVE, "Dict. of Music," ii; 500.

The search for an earlier example of the opera than the "Siege of Rhodes" rewards the curious only by regarding the letter rather than the spirit. "In 1617 Nicolo Laniere set an entire Masque of Ben Jonson's to music, in the *Stilo recitativo*, and may therefore justly claim the credit of having composed the first English Opera, though he was by birth an Italian. But the practice was not continued." — GROVE, ii; 507.

The transition from masque to opera was not complete even in Purcell's day. Dryden styled "Albion and Albanius," produced 1685, published 1691, an opera, and yet, as Professor Saintsbury says, "it is not easy to see why Dryden should not have kept the ancient name of Masque for the piece, — a name which thoroughly fits it." Sir Walter Scott thus comments: "Our author appears to have found it difficult to assign a name for this performance, which was at once to address itself to the eye, the ear, and the understanding. The ballad-opera, since invented, in which part is sung, part acted and spoken, comes nearest to its description." Dryden also called the "State of Innocence" an opera, but the appropriateness of the title has been denied on the ground that it "contains no lyrical poetry, the music employed in it being entirely instrumental." — HOGARTH, i; 83. In another instance Dryden seems to be at a loss for a name. "It cannot properly be called a play, because the action of it is supposed to be conducted sometimes by supernatural means, or magick; nor an opera, because the story of it is not sung." (Preface to "Albion and Albanius.") Nevertheless Dryden has his own notions on the species which in the same preface he defended against imaginary opponents:

"An opera is a poetical tale, or fiction, represented by vocal and instrumental music, adorned with scenes, machines, and dancing. The supposed persons of this musical drama are generally supernatural, as gods and goddesses and heroes, which at least are descended from them, and are in due time to be adopted into their number. The subject, therefore, being extended beyond the limits of human nature, admits of that sort of marvellous and surprising conduct, which is rejected in other plays. Human impossibilities are to be received as they are in faith; because, where gods are introduced, a supreme power is to be understood, and second causes are out of doors. Yet propriety is to be observed even here. The gods are all to manage their own peculiar provinces; and what was attributed by the heathens to one power ought not to be performed by any other. Phœbus must foretell, Mercury must charm with his caduceus, and Juno must reconcile the quarrels of the marriage-bed. To conclude, they must all act according to their distinct and peculiar characters. If the persons represented were to speak upon the stage it would follow of necessity that the expressions should be lofty, figurative, and majestical; but the nature of an opera denies the frequent use of these poetical ornaments; for vocal music, though it often admits a loftiness of sound, yet always exacts an harmonious sweetness; or, to distinguish yet more justly, the recitative part of the opera requires a more masculine beauty of expression and sound; the other, which, for want of a proper English word, I must call the *songish part*, must abound in the softness and variety of numbers; its principal intention being to please hearing rather than to gratify the understanding . . . I said . . . that the persons represented in operas are generally gods, goddesses, and heroes descended from them, who are supposed to be their peculiar care; which hinders not, but that meaner persons may sometimes be gracefully introduced, especially if they have relation to those first times, which poets call the Golden Age; wherein, by reason of their innocence, those happy mortals were supposed to have had a more familiar intercourse with superior beings; and, therefore, shepherds might reasonably be admitted as of all callings the most innocent, the most happy, and who, by reason of the spare time they had, in their almost idle employment, had most leisure to make verses, and to be in love; without somewhat of which passion, no opera can possibly subsist."

From the foregoing extract it will be observed that Dryden's conception of opera and of the heroic drama (stated in his "Essay on Heroic Plays") is the same in the following respects: the characters, if human, are to be heroic (in the original sense — approaching demi-gods); the improbable is justifiable; and as love (with valor) is the subject of the one, without it no opera can possibly subsist. The points of divergence, on the other hand, are in the diction; in the fact that most of the characters in the former are either supernatural or of low birth, whereas in the heroic play they come from neither of these "social spheres"; and in the opera's "principal intention being to please hearing rather than to gratify understanding."

It is this last consideration — that the opera did not appeal to the understanding — that is at the root of Dryden's contempt for the office of librettist. He chafes under the yoke and swears he will never be a slave to the composition again:

"The same reasons which depress thought in an opera, have a stronger effect upon the words, especially in our language; for there is no maintaining the purity of English in short measures, where the rhyme returns so quick, and it is so often female, or double rhyme, which is not natural to our tongue, because it consists too much of monosyllables, and those too most commonly clogged with consonants; for which reason I am often forced to coin new words, revive some that are antiquated, and botch others, as if I had not served out my time in poetry, but was bound apprentice to some doggerel rhymer, who makes songs to tunes, and sings them for a livelihood. It is true I have not been often put to this drudgery; but where I have, the words will sufficiently shew that I was then a slave to the composition, which I will never be again; it is my part to invent, and the musicians to humour that invention. I may be counselled, and will always follow my friend's advice where I find it reasonable, but will never part with the power of the militia." — Preface to "Albion and Albanius."

But he spoke too soon, and did not keep his resolution. And while there appears good enough evidence of the friendship between Dryden and Purcell at the time the following extract from the Dedication to "King Arthur," 1691, was written, his disrespect for the matter in hand is none the less evident because instead of being openly expressed, as previously in the preface to "Albion and Albanius," it is now subtly and deftly insinuated with that affected satisfaction with his age which he so frequently assumed and could so easily throw off.

"I humbly offer you this trifle, which, if it succeed upon the stage, is like to be the chiefest entertainment of our ladies and gentlemen this summer. When I wrote it, seven years ago, I employed some reading about it, to inform myself out of Beda, Bochartus, and other authors, concerning the rites and customs of the heathen Saxons; as I also used the little skill I have in poetry to adorn it. But not to offend the present times, nor a government which has hitherto protected me, I have been obliged so much to alter the first design, and take away so many beauties from the writing, that it is now no more what it was formerly, than the present ship of the Royal Sovereign, after so often taking down and altering, is the vessel it was at the first building. There is nothing better than what I intended, but the musick, which has since arrived to a greater perfection in England than ever formerly; especially passing through the artful hands of Mr. Purcell, who has composed it with so great a genius, that he has nothing to fear but an ignorant, ill-judging audience.

"But the numbers of poetry and vocal musick are sometimes so contrary, that in many places I have been obliged to cramp my verses, and make them rugged to the reader, that they may be harmonious to the hearer; of which I have no reason to repent me, because these sorts of entertainments are principally designed for the ear and eye; and therefore, in reason, my art on this occasion ought to be subservient to his. And besides, I flatter myself with an imagination, that a judicious audience will easily distinguish betwixt the songs wherein I have complied with him, and those in which I have followed the rules of poetry in the sound and cadence of the words."

A successful, though highly unesteemed contemporary also speaks contemptuously and without reserve of the office of librettist:

"In a thing written in five weeks, . . . there must needs be many ERROURS, which . . . I have not had leisure to mend, . . . nor would it indeed be worth the Pains, since there are as many Objects in the Play, and such variety of Diversion, as will not give the Audience leave to mind the Writing; and I doubt not but the Candid Reader will forgive the faults when he considers that the great Design was to entertain the Town with variety of Musick, curious Dancing, splendid Scenes and Machines; and that

I do not, nor ever did intend to value myself upon the writing of this Play. For I had rather be Author of one Scene of Comedy, like some of Ben Johnson's, than of all the best plays of this kind that have been, or ever shall be written; Good Comedy requiring much more Wit and Judgment in the Writer, than any rhyming, unnatural Plays can do. This I have so little valued that I have not alter'd six lines in it since it was first written, which (except the songs at the Marriage of Psyche in the last Scene) was all done sixteen months since. In all the Words which are sung, I did not so much take care of the Wit or Fancy of 'em, as the making of 'em proper for musick; in which I cannot but have some little knowledge, having been bred for many years of my Youth to some Performance in it.

"I chalked out the way to the Composer (in all but the Song of Furies and Devils in the Fifth Act), having designed which Line I would have sung by One, which by Two, which by Three, which by four Voices, &c., and what manner of humour I would have in all the Vocal Musick." — SHADWELL'S "Psyche," Preface.

The presence of operatic features meant chiefly a greater attention than in the drama proper to the spectacular. There appears little doubt that it was the opinion of certain playwrights and critics that in proportion to the importance of the operatic element the significance and dignity of the dramatist's function decreased. Dryden and Shadwell have been cited; and among contemporary theatre-goers Langbaine gives a curt account of the popular success of "Psyche" — a work most vehemently damned by the critics. "How much this Opera takes, every Body that is acquainted with the Theatre knows;

and with reason, since the greatest Masters in Vocal Musick, Dancing, and Painting, were concern'd in it." There is also Wright's testimony.—"Historia Histronica," 1699:

"It is an argument of the worth of the plays and actors of the last age, and easily inferred, that they were much beyond ours in this, to consider that they could support themselves merely from their own merit, the weight of the matter, and goodness of the action, without scenes and machines; whereas the present plays with all that shew can hardly draw an audience, unless there be the additional invitation of a Signior Fideli, a Monsieur l'Abbe, or some such foreign regale expressed in the bottom of the bill."

These facts naturally lead to a questioning of Mr. E. Sutherland Edwards's opinion: "It never occurred to the dramatists of the Restoration that there was anything in the opera that could interfere with the well-being of the spoken drama" ("Lyrical Drama," ii; 123–124); but rather to a crediting of the statement (Ward, iii; 320) which called it forth: "The complaints of our dramatists are both loud and deep as to the difficulty which they experienced in maintaining a struggle against" the opera.

It has been questioned whether contemporaries were warranted in their belief that the importation of operatic features was detrimental to dramatic art. Professor Ward (iii; 330) agrees with them: "The Opera usurped so large a share of fashionable favour that the progress of the English drama could not fail to suffer from the success of this foreign importation on the boards of English theatres." But Mr. Edwards is on the negative side:

"It can be shown by historical evidence . . . that opera has never injured the drama." — "Lyrical Drama," ii; 122.

Any discussion of opera *versus* drama of this era is primarily a matter of the extent to which the latter depended for its maintenance upon features that did not appeal directly to the understanding. Such features were vocal and instrumental music, dancing, costume and scenery, and their combination is commonly called operatic. The connotation of this adjective has always assigned a leading place to the spectacular element. The meaning of the noun "opera" has somewhat changed. The modern use of the word refers primarily and perhaps almost solely to the presence of music, because owing to the continued and ever growing resort to stage accessories by the drama proper, they are no longer considered peculiarly characteristic of the opera. But in the seventeenth century opera meant mainly "scenes and machines," and the musical element, if it was introduced at all, was, as a rule, comparatively unimportant. Langbaine's few words rather corroborate such an assumption, and Genest (i; 139) expressly says; "Downes considers Machinery so essential to an Opera, that he calls (Shadwell's) 'Lancashire Witches' (1681) a kind of Opera, because there were machines for the Witches."

The opera was in its infancy. No one knew exactly what it was, because it had not attained sufficient growth, and was in such a pliable condition that any definition of one day might be obsolete the next. There was no opera house in London, nor one even exclusively given over to spectacular productions, for although the Dorset Gardens was erected for that sort of entertainment, and was perhaps chiefly devoted to such use, yet the managers of that play-house were by no means averse to putting on a tragedy or a comedy in which little stage adornment of any kind was required. Likewise, although Sir W. Davenant's theatre, from his early association with the term, may have been popularly known as the opera, yet that does not seem to have been its official name, nor would there have been much appropriateness in such a title considering the general character of its productions. There was no opera-going, as distinct from a theatre-going, public; there was no rage for the opera such as characterized the beginning of the succeeding century, for the manifest reason that, of opera pure and simple, there was next to none.

The number of so-called operas — so-called by their authors — produced or printed in the confines of our period was not large, but small, hardly appreciable in comparison with the hundreds of various sorts of dramatic compositions then written. The "Siege of Rhodes," called an opera in its first and incomplete form during the Commonwealth, was elaborately produced as such in 1662. Cambert's and Grafue's opera of "Ariadne," a translation from the French, was produced in 1674. Thus twelve years elapsed between the first and second opera; the second was, moreover, a court production. "Albion and Albanius" was given in the year of Charles II.'s death, and "King Arthur" in 1691. "Cassandra" (1692), and "Fairy Queen" (1692), are far less known. Both are anonymous. The latter is an adaptation of "Midsummer Night's Dream," and is prefixed by a defence of the opera. At the very end of the century are Durfey's "Cynthia and Endymion" (1697) and "Brutus of Alba" (1697), published by Powell and Verbruggen, and stolen from Tate's tragedy of the same name; Settle's "World in the Moon" (1697), and Motteux's adaptation of

Fletcher's "Island Princess" (1699). If the "Biographia Dramatica" is to be relied upon when the original itself is not at command, these were all called operas. Two others, not intended for the stage, are Dryden's "State of Innocence" (1676), and a sequel to it, Ecclestton's "Noah's Flood" (1679). Alexis's "Paradise" (1680) and Betterton's adaptation of Fletcher's "Prophetess" (1690) were styled dramatic operas.

This list comprises, so far as can be ascertained from a study of Baker and Holliwell, all the self-styled operas given to the world in one form or another from 1656 to 1702. "Pastor Fido," in the form of Settle's translation of 1677, "a pastoral," probably should be placed in this class. A Restoration operatic form of the "Tempest" was called a comedy, and some so-called tragedies, of which Shadwell's "Psyche" (1674) and Charles Davenant's "Circe" (1677) were popular successful examples, were as thoroughly operatic as the operas in name.

The smallness of the list would indicate that the authors — doubtless because of the formlessness of the kind — did not like to call their works operas, and that the word was not as yet in common use. Still the list reveals a comparatively goodly number of Elizabethan plays made over, and improved, as was thought, by the introduction of scenes and machines. Some of these alterations deviated from the original much more than others, but in all cases what was added was, in short, the operatic element; and the boasted purpose unquestionably was to illustrate the advance in stage mechanism by challenging a comparison unfavorable to the preceding age. The list shows, furthermore, that the genesis of English opera was in tragedy. It had, in its earliest form, a serious theme, and it was not until the close of the century in 1697, that the "World in the Moon" appeared, — an early example, if not, indeed, the first, of what was to be comic opera. Gildon, who took up Langbaine's work, remarked the change. "This is something unusual," said he, "being a comical Opera."

It is plain that as the study of the heroic play necessitates a determination of the heroic element in various dramatic forms, to an even greater extent a study of seventeenth-century English opera cannot deal primarily with so-called opera, but must be rather an account of the infusion and diffusion of the operatic element in Restoration plays. This element affected many heroic plays, and yet some of the most typical instances of the heroic kind seem to have been, in so far as may be ascertained through the play itself and the stage directions, in the absence of external evidence, non-operatic. Such are "Herod and Mariamne," "Siege of Babylon," "Tryphon," and "Ibrahim"; the dignified "Mustapha," of which Pepys said, "a most excellent play for words and design, as ever I did see"; one of Betterton's successes, the "English Princess"; and the highly lauded "Don Carlos."

There is good reason for the existence of the operatic element in Restoration tragedies. In them the background is of war: the hero wooes in armor, the battle-call impends. Thus the subject invites military display and martial music. They must have been literally noisy, the drum much heard. Dryden in his "Essay on Heroic Plays" advocates noise and fighting:

"To those who object my frequent use of drums and trumpets, and my representation of battles; I answer, I introduced them not on the English stage; Shakespeare used them frequently; and though Jonson shows no battle in his 'Catiline,' yet you hear from behind the scenes the sounding of trumpets, and the shouts of fighting armies. But, I add further, that these warlike instruments, and even their presentation of fighting on the stage, are no more than necessary to produce the effects of an heroic play."

The characters were royal as well as martial, and therefore richness of costume and scenery was appropriate, and afforded an opportunity to the costumer and the scene-painter. The visible appearance of the supernatural was common; devils, ghosts, and spirits of all kinds abounded, and thus the ingenuity of the stage carpenter was exercised in the construction of machines. Then there was dancing, and its rise and popularity in England as a form of theatrical attraction was of course contemporaneous with the introduction of women on the stage; and so there was a demand for dancing-masters. A great many of the serious plays contained one or more of these elements, and owed their success in part to the costumer, stage-carpenter, scene-painter, dancing-master, and musician.

Shadwell, in the preface to "Psyche," appears to have acknowledged this indebtedness more frankly than any other of his contemporaries:

"All the instrumental musick (which is not mingled with the vocal) was composed by that great master, Seignior Gio. Baptista Draghi, Master of the Italian Musick to the King. The dances were made by the most famous master of France, Monsieur St. Andree. The Scenes were painted by the ingenious artist, Mr. Stephenson. In those things that concern the Ornament or Decoration of the Play, the great Industry and Care of Mr. Betterton ought to be remembered, at whose desire I wrote upon this subject."

There were many plays in which operatic features, although present, were of little consequence. Such are "Destruction of Troy," "Great Favorite," "Marcelia," "Rival Kings," and "Siege of Memphis." There were others which would admit of such features, and yet now naught but the words remain, and it is difficult to determine to what extent other features entered — so fleeting are the names and things that make for theatrical rather than for dramatic success. There are still others wherein the gorgeousness of their production has become stage-legend, wherein also their total effect and success were largely due to external means rather than, and sometimes in spite of, their dramatic quality. Settle's "Empress of Morocco" was one — wondrously staged, immediately successful, arousing discussion and enmity, and dramatically without merit. Most of Dryden's heroic plays depended partly for their success upon externals; although amazing literary achievements, they were produced with all the advantages of accessories that the theatre possessed. In them there was considerable music which was important, although incidental, and the fact that Purcell composed for "Indian Emperor," "Indian Queen," "Aureng-Zebe," and "Tyrannic Love" (Hogarth claims that the last-named piece was made less absurd by the beauty of the music than it would otherwise have been) has assured their permanence in the annals of another art besides literature. Dryden further admits, in the "Essay" above referred to, that he is not at all ashamed of resorting to stage devices: "That the Red Bull has formerly done the same, . . . is no more an argument against our practice than it would be for a physician to forebear an approved medicine, because a montebank has used it with success."

Lovers of literature usually claim that the combination of literature and music is pernicious to their art, for although a lyric independently written may then be set to music so happily that the two become inseparably associated, the conscious writing of words to suit music already composed is frequently incompatible with the natural expression of poetic genius. Dryden's disrespect for the opera was partly due to his appreciation of this fact. Ward, as a historian, thus insists on the literary worthlessness of operas: "Few English dramatic works possessing any literary importance are included among the contributions to this hybrid species." And Addison was so impressed with the incompatibility of the two arts that he came to the conclusion that "nothing is capable of being set to music that is not nonsense."

So the influence of opera upon the heroic play and upon Restoration drama in general, refers only secondarily to the relation between literature and music, to the introduction of a new art into the previously peculiar field of the spoken drama. But in the main it means nothing more nor less than a hitherto unprecedented recognition of the numerous and varied features that make for theatrical effectiveness; and whereas they were from the beginning considered under the broad head "operatic," they antedated, in fact, that set art-form which distinguished the early years of the eighteenth century,—a form which owed little to its early English counterpart. "It was perfectly true that, at that time 'our English music was quite rooted out.' . . . Purcell, though not twenty years dead, was as clean forgotten as if he had never been." — HOGARTH, i; 218.

The eighteenth century, moreover, witnessed the decline of both music and opera: "What hope or expectation then can the public entertain of receiving that rational, that irreproachable delight which the theatre is capable of affording us through the medium of music? If managers know not what it is, and if it is not to be known through the theatre, much less, heaven knows, is it to be known through the opera; a spectacle where the dance is the plot and the opera the episode; but remarks of this complexion will come better after I have gone through an account of music, which, during forty years, grew into the highest perfection in this country, and is now sunk into insignificance." — DIBDIN (1795), V; 213.

At the Restoration arose the question which has lasted to the present day, as to the legitimacy of the dramatic poets permitting or inviting the introduction of parts that appealed primarily to the eye and the ear rather than to the understanding for the attainment of a definite object. Although Dryden did not believe in operatic features supplanting the play proper in importance, he approved the introduction of externals for the purpose of helping the verisimilitude. He says in the "Essay": They "are no more than necessary to produce the effects of an heroic play; that is, to raise the imagination of the audience, and to persuade them, for the time, that what they behold on the theatre is really performed. The poet is then to endeavour an absolute dominion over the minds of the spectators, for though our fancy will contribute to its own deceit, yet a writer ought to help its operation."

Gildon(?) (Life of Betterton, p. 6) is of the same opinion: "Tho this be affirm'd by some, others have laid it to the Charge of Mr. Betterton as the first Innovator on our rude Stage, as a Crime; nay as the Destruction of good Playing; but I think with very little Show of Reason. . . . For how that which helps the Representation by assisting the pleasing Delusion of the Mind in regard of the place, should spoil the Acting, I cannot imagine." On the other hand, this growing tendency had its censors.

It may be difficult to free the mind from the conviction that attention to the externals of stage-craft is inimical to the fullest exercise of the imagination, so deep-rooted is the modern credence in the superior keenness of the Elizabethan audience in this regard over all its successors. It would seem that, necessarily, absence of stage-adornment must have concentrated the attention to a degree since unequalled upon the thought of the writer and upon the actor's delivery. Nevertheless, the change from a barren to a furnished stage was inevitable, as was also the change from the conception that a play was made by the partnership of poet and actor to the conception of it as a product of the harmonious combination of several arts; and there is danger of over-estimating the deleterious effects of this combination. For the play, after all, remains the thing, and there have been other great actors than and since Burbage. The player's art was still an art in the eighteenth century, and the decline of tragedy, if it was at all related to the rise of stage-craft, certainly was not brought about principally by that rise. At any rate, evidence seems to be wanting that the rhyming dramatists of the Restoration were controlled to any marked extent by the presence of operatic features. Such features were not inherent but incidental, and not invariable, as there are plays of the same species with and without them. And that they do not determine the species is indicated by the similarity of the plays with this element to those without it.

The operatic and heroic elements existed side by side

with strangely little directing power over each other. As the century advanced, a few men of pronounced ability, with a liking for manners and satire, succeeded in perpetuating their own taste and that of their times by the composition of so-called Restoration comedy. But the flowering time of Restoration tragedy was earlier — in the reign of Charles II. Both products indicate a greater interest in what appealed to the understanding than these forty years of dramatic activity are usually credited with. There are no English plays that are more coldly intellectual than Congreve's, and heroic plays were intended to make an intellectual appeal; the long rhymed speeches indicate an attention real or affected in the art of delivery; and the frequency of argumentation, a liking for a certain kind of mental exercise.

Therefore, although it is true that operatic features entered into most heroic plays, the primary distinction of appealing to the understanding always existed, and the heroic element, while it lasted, continued true to its ideals.

APPENDIX B

A BRIEF SURVEY OF THREE HEROIC PLAYS IN OUTLINE, AS CONTRASTED WITH SHAKESPEARE

SHAKESPEARE'S KING RICHARD III

DRAMATIS PERSONÆ

King Edward the Fourth,
Edward, Prince of Wales, afterward King Edward V, } sons to the king.
Richard, Duke of York, }
George, Duke of Clarence, } brothers to the king.
Richard, Duke of Gloucester, afterward King Richard III, }
A young son of Clarence.
Henry, Earl of Richmond, afterward King Henry VII.
Cardinal Bourchier, Archbishop of Canterbury.
Thomas Rotherham, Archbishop of York.
John Morton, Bishop of Ely.
Duke of Buckingham.
Duke of Norfolk.
Earl of Surrey, his son.
Earl Rivers, brother to Elizabeth.
Marquis of Dorset and Lord Grey, sons to Elizabeth.
Earl of Oxford.
Lord Hastings.
Lord Stanley, called also Earl of Derby.
Lord Lovel.
Sir Thomas Vaughan.
Sir Richard Ratcliff.
Sir William Catesby.

Sir James Tyrrel.
Sir James Blount.
Sir Walter Herbert.
Sir Robert Brakenbury, Lieutenant of the Tower.
Christopher Urswick, a priest. Another priest.
Tressel and Berkeley, gentlemen attending on the Lady Anne.
Lord Mayor of London. Sheriff of Wiltshire.
Elizabeth, queen to King Edward IV.
Margaret, widow of King Henry VI.
Duchess of York, mother to King Edward IV.
Lady Anne, widow of Edward, Prince of Wales, son to King Henry VI: afterward married to Richard.
A young daughter of Clarence (Margaret Plantagenet).
Ghosts of those murdered by Richard III, Lords and other attendants; a Pursuivant, Scrivener, Citizens, Murderers, Messengers, Soldiers, etc.

CARYL'S (?) ENGLISH PRINCESS

THE PERSONS

King Richard the Third.
Queen Dowager of Edward the Fourth.
Princess Elizabeth, daughter of Edward the Fourth.
Earl of Richmond, Crown'd Henry the Seventh.
Earl of Oxford.
Lord Stanly.
Lord Strange, his son.
Lord Chanden of Bretany.
Sir William Stanley.
Charlot, page to the Princess.
Lord Lovel.
Sir William Catesby.
Sir Richard Ratclife.
Miles Forrest.
The Prior of Litchfield.
A Captain, a Lieutenant, Souldiers, Guards, and Attendants.

OUTLINE OF THE PLOT

Act I

Richard the Third desires for his wife, Princess Elizabeth, daughter of Henry the Fourth, who is engaged to Earl of Richmond, crowned Henry the Seventh. He commissions Sir William Stanley to advance his cause. Elizabeth's mother, the queen, advises the princess to accept Richard, but she refuses to do so.

Act II

Concerns the relation of minor characters, particularly Sir William Stanley, to the main plot, and the story of Charlot, the page.

Act III

Scene between the princess and the king, in which he, after wooing in vain, says he will see to her death. First appearance of Richmond in his camp. Enter a prior, who prophesies for him success in love and war.

Act IV

Description of scene in the camp of both Richmond and the king. Richmond resolves to visit the princess the night before the battle, which he does. The king has a dream in which he sees the ghosts of those he has murdered.

Act V

Richmond kills the king and successfully wooes the princess.

The above is the main story of this play. The principal under-stories are those (1) of Charlot and (2) Sir William Stanley. Charlot is the runaway daughter of Lord Chanden, of Bretany, in Richmond's army. She falls in love with Richmond, is disguised as a boy,—page to the princess,—carries love messages from the earl to the princess, and remains so true to her higher self, that in the last act she has the princess change costumes with her that danger may fall upon herself if detected. She finally retires to a monastery. (2) Sir William Stanley hopelessly loves the princess. In the last act, as a matter of self-sacrifice, he disguises himself as Richmond, in order to deceive Richard, thus successfully helping Richmond in his victory.

The following song (Act III, Sc. 4) is in character with the prevailing atmosphere of the play.

SONG

I

"Tyrant, thou seek'st in vain
With her pure Blood thy guilty Sword to stain;
Heaven does that Sacred Blood design
To be the Source of an Immortal Line.
Death will not dare to touch that Heart,
Which Love has chosen for his dart.

Chorus

Fair Innocence and Beauty are
Of watchful Heaven the chiefest care;
But the devouring Monster shall
A sacrifice to Justice fall.

II

Richmond does flye to your Redress;
(Love's Messenger can do no less.)
His Sword shall with one Blow
Cut off your Fetters and the Tyrant too.
All Resistance vain will prove
When Valour is inspir'd by Love.

Chorus

Tyrants' by Heaven and Earth are curst;
They swell with Blood untill they burst;
But Lovers are wise Nature's care;
What Tyrants ruine they repair."

SHAKESPEARE'S ANTONY AND CLEOPATRA

DRAMATIS PERSONÆ

Mark Antony,
Octavius Cæsar,
M. Æmelius Lepidus, } triumvirs.

Demitius Enobarbus,
Ventidius,
Eros,
Scarus,
Dercetas,
Demetrius,
Philo, } friends to Antony.

Mecænas,
Agrippa,
Dolabella,
Proculeius,
Thyreus,
Gallus. } friends to Cæsar.

Menas, | friends to Pompey.
Menecrates,
Varrius.

Taurus, lieutenant-general to Cæsar.
Canidius, lieutenant-general to Antony.
Silius, an officer in Ventidius's army.
Euphronius, an ambassador from Antony to Cæsar.

Alexas, | attendants on Cleopatra.
Mardian, a Eunuch,
Selucus,
Diomedes,

A Soothsayer. A Clown.
Cleopatra, queen of Egypt.
Octavia, sister to Cæsar and wife to Antony.

Charmian, | attendants on Cleopatra.
Iras,

Officers, Soldiers, Messengers, and other attendants.

SEDLEY'S ANTONY AND CLEOPATRA

PERSONS REPRESENTED

Cæsar.
Agrippa.
Mecænas.
Lucilius, a Roman.
Thyreus.
Antony.
Canidius.
Photinus.
Memnon, | two Egyptian Lords.
Chilax.
Cleopatra.
Octavia.
Iras.
Charmion.

Guards, Messengers, Villains, Souldiers, and Attendants, Men and Women.

OUTLINE OF THE PLOT

ACT I

Description of state of affairs after the sea-fight; Antony controlled by Cleopatra; Hatred of Egyptian Lords for him; Roman friends advise him to fight and save his honor.

Act II

Photinus, Cæsar's spy, evidently an Egyptian who loves Iras, seeks through proving false to Antony and friendly to Cæsar, to gain Antony's throne and have his love for Iras rewarded, as she promises. Mecænas advises Cæsar to take harsh measures against Antony, and tells Octavia he thus acts because of love for her, which learning she commands him in the name of that love to cease.

Act III

Thyreus, ambassador from Rome, offers peace; he has a private interview with Cleopatra, in which he tells her not to fear for herself whatever becomes of Antony. He makes love to Cleopatra, and they are discovered by Antony. Cleopatra claims innocence. The army shout for Thyreus's release.

Act IV

Octavia accuses Cæsar of taking harsh measures against Antony, not for love of her as he feigned, but for ambition.

Antony kills Thyreus and learns of Cleopatra's innocence from him. Photinus discovered in his treachery, yet pardoned by Antony who is victorious.

Act V

Cæsar victorious. News brought to Antony. Photinus in order to get Antony out of the way tells him Cleopatra is dead. Antony thereupon wounds himself. Lucilius declines to be instrumental in his lord's death and kills himself. Antony dies in Cleopatra's arms. Cleopatra takes unto herself an asp. Charmion does likewise, first applying it to Iras who would live. All then die. On which scene Cæsar and his men enter. Photinus consummates the death of Iras, on which Iras' brother kills him.

There are two scenes which are representative of Restoration treatment of a tragedy theme: one is a love meeting between Antony and the Egyptian (Act I, Sc. 2), and the other is Antony's death (Act V).

"*Cleop.* For you my Peoples love and more I lost,
Must I not keep what has so dearly cost?
Ant. Ah Madam, you shou'd take the weakest part,
And help a Lover to defend his Heart,
Tho swounding Men with ease resign their Breath,
Their careful Friends still pull 'm back from Death.
You should my Lethargy of Honour chide,
And drive me tho unwilling, from your side.
Die at your feet the meanest Lover might,
But in your quarrel the whole World shall fight.
Cleop. If I am Captive to the *Romans* made;
Surpriz'd in this weak place, or else betray'd;
Think not I'le live to be redeem'd again,
And like a Slave of my proud Lords complain.
At the first Dawn of my ill Fate I'le die.
Ant. O name not Death we'l meet in Triumph here:
I'le raise the Siege e're you have time to fear.
Cleop. But then your Love, in absence, will it last?
Men think of joys to come, and slight the past.
Ant. My Heart shall like those Trees that East does show,
Where Blossoms and ripe Fruit hang on one Bough.
With new desires, soft hopes, at once be prest;
And all those Riper Joys, Love gives the blest.

Courage and Love shall sway each in their turn,
I'le fight to conquer, conquer to return.
Seeming Ambitious to the publick view,
I'le make my private end and dearer, You.
This Storm once past; in Peace and Love we'l Raign,
Like the Immortal Gods, the Giants slain.

Cleop. Moments to absent Lovers tedious grow;
'Tis not how time, but how the mind does go.
And once *Antonius* wou'd have thought so too.

Ant. Dearer than ever think not that I part,
Without the utmost Torment of my Heart.
Whil'st you perswade, your danger chides me stay,
Make me not cast me and your Self away.
How well I lov'd, you did at *Actium* see,
When to be near you I left Victory.
And chose to be companion of your flight,
Rather than conquer in a distant Fight.
Press not that heart you know so well, too far,
Our Fortune will no second frailty bear.

Cleop. The truest Misers choose to sit about,
And tell their wealth: but dare not trust it out.
I know as well as you, 'tis fit you go,
Yet what is best I cannot let you do.

Ant. For my attendance I some few will take;
All other *Romans* of your Guard I make.

Cleop. If you must go, it quickly shall appear,
My love sought this delay, and not my fear.
When you attaque, we'l sally from the Town,
And blood instead of *Nile* our Plain shall drown.
We'l in the midst of *Cæsar's* Army meet,
And like *Bellona* I my *Mars* will greet.

Ant. Wou'd Goddesses themselves to me endear,
In *Cleopatra's* shape they must appear.

Cleop. My heart can danger though not absence bear,
To Love, 'tis Wax, but Adamant to Fear.
Ant. Mine has such Courage from your Firmness took,
That I can almost bear a parting look.
Cleop. Take it; and each unto their charge make haste.
Ant. Our hardest victory I hope is past.
Exeunt omnes."

Enter ANTONIUS, CLEOPATRA, CHARMION *and* IRAS

In the Monument

"*Anto.* 'Twas I that pull'd on you the hate of *Rome*,
And all your Ills, past, present, and to come.
It is not fit nor possible I live,
And my dear Queen, it growes unkind to grieve.
Cleop. 'Twas I that lost you in each *Roman* mind;
And to your ruine can you still be kind?
How can you bear this Tyranny of Fate,
And not the cause, your *Cleopatra* hate.
Anto. So Venus look't, when the *Idalian* boar
The tender side of her *Adonis* tore;
Nor yields my Queen in Beauty or in grief,
When half the World under my rule was plac't
Your love was all the joy that I cou'd tast,
It was my chief delight, and is my last.
I dye, and have but one short word to say;
But you must swear, my Queen you will obey.
Cleop. By all our love I will my death command,
And see the eager duty of my hand.
Anto. Your death! it is the only thing I fear;
And Fate no other way can reach me here.
Cleop. Down from a throne to any private State;

It is a dismal Precipice to the Great.
I giddy with the horrid prospect grow;
And shall fall in, unless Death help me now.

Anto. Heav'n that success does to my Arms deny,
Whispers a *Roman* Soul, and bids him dye.
Our case is different; to Cæsar sue,
Tho me he hate, he needs must pity you.
Your Beauty and my Love were all your Crime,
And you must live my Queen.

Cleop. When you are dead —
To be despis'd, reproach't, in triumph lead;
A Queen and Slave! who wou'd not life renounce,
Rather than bear those distant names at once.

Anto. But you may live a Queen; say you obey'd
Through fear; and were compelled to give me aid;
That all your Subjects private orders had
Not to resist him, and my Cause betray'd.
Say, that at last you did my death procure;
Say anything that may your Life and Crown secure.

Cleop. 'Twere false and base, it rather shall be said
I kill'd myself when I beheld you dead.

Anto. Me the unhappy cause of all your wo!
Your own, and your dear Country's overthrow.
Remember I was jealous, rash, soon mov'd,
Suspected no less fiercely than I lov'd;
How I *Thyreus* kill'd, your Love accus'd,
And to your kind defence my faith refus'd.
From shame and rage I soon shall be at rest,
And Death of thousand ills hath chose the best.

[*He faints.*

Cleop. O stay! and take me with you.

Anto. Dearest Queen,
Let my Life end before your Death begin.

O *Rome!* thy freedom does with me expire,
And thou art left, obtaining thy desire." [*Dies.*

Antony says (Act II, Sc. 2) that he married Octavia to avert a "growing storm."

"*Cleop.* O my Antonius! how I fear this Peace!
And must I to Octavia yield my place?
I love you so, that very sound wou'd kill,
And leave you free the promise to fulfil.
Ant. Were I to gain the Empire of mankind,
And for that pow'r Eternity assign'd;
I cou'd not to the hateful change submit,
Nor my best Queen so barbarously quit.
Cleop. But your Octavia, loving, young, and fair,
And such a Rival! how can I but fear?
Ant. Her Hymen never did a Moment please,
The hard Condition of a needful Peace;
From every part I saw the growing storm,
A sudden shelter in her arms I took,
Which when 'twas over I again forsook."

And he excuses his present conduct thus:

"From past engagements, present Love, set free.
Hymen is but the Vulgars Deity."

One, to whom Hymen is but the Vulgars Deity, would naturally think well of Cleopatra's virtue.

"T' attempt the spotless Honor of my Queen,
Is such a Crime, as it is death to mean."
(Act IV, Sc. 4.)

Though Cleopatra is not popularly regarded for her spotless honor, yet mention of it is not entirely unprecedented. Cf. Chaucer's "Legend of Good Women":

"This noble quene eek lovede so this knight,
Through his desert, and for his chivalrye,
As certainly, but — if that bokes lye,
He was of persone and of gentilesse,
And of discrecioun and hardiness,
Worthy to any wight that liven may,
And she was fair as is the rose in May.
And, for to maken shortly is the beste,
She wex his wyf, and hadde him as her leste."

SHAKESPEARE'S HENRY FIFTH

PERSONS REPRESENTED

King Henry the Fifth.
Duke of Gloucester, } brothers to the King.
Duke of Bedford, }
Duke of Exeter, uncle to the King.
Duke of York, cousin to the King.
Earls of Salisbury, Westmoreland, and Warwick.
Archbishop of Canterbury.
Bishop of Ely.
Earl of Cambridge, }
Lord Scroop, } conspirators against the King.
Sir Thomas Grey, }
Sir Thomas Erpingham, Gower, Fluellen, Macmorris, Jamy, officers in King Henry's army.
Bates, Court, Williams, soldiers in the same.
Nym, Bardolph, Pistol, formerly servants to Falstaff, now soldiers in the same.
Boy, servant to them.
A herald.
Chorus.
Charles the Sixth, King of France.
Lewis, the Dauphin.
Dukes of Burgundy, Orleans, and Bourbon.

The Constable of France.
Rambures and Grandpre, French lords.
Governor of Harfleur.
Montjoy, a French herald.
Ambassadors to the King of England.
Isabel, Queen of France.
Katharine, daughter to Charles and Isabel.
Alice, a lady attending on the Princess Katharine.
Quickly, Pistol's wife, an hostess.
Lords, Ladies, Officers, French and English Soldiers, Messengers and Attendants.

ORRERY'S HENRY FIFTH

PERSONS

Henry the Fifth.
Duke of Bedford.
Duke of Exeter.
Earl of Warwick.
Owen Tudor.
Archbishop of Canterbury.
The Dauphin.
Duke of Burgundy.
Constable of France.
Bishop of Arras.
Earl of Charoloys.
Count de Chastel.
Count de Blaumont.
Monsier Colemore.

WOMEN

Queen of France.
Princess Katharine.
Princess Anne of Burgundy.
Countess of La Mar.
A French Lady.

OUTLINE OF THE PLOT

ACT I

The war between France and England—then Tudor's love for Katharine related by herself, and Bedford's love for Anne by herself.

Act II

This may be divided into three parts. (1) The king informs his courtiers of his terms of peace to France and of his love for Katharine. (2) The queen debates with her courtiers whether to yield to England or not. (3) Tudor, the lover of Katharine, expresses to Katharine the king's love for her, and is made to understand that his own case is hopeless.

Act III

The political position of the Duke of Burgundy described. The king visits Katharine incognito, discovers himself, and both are discovered by the Dauphin, whom the king disarms. Katharine shows the king means of escape.

Act IV

Unsuccessful peace negotiations between French and English. Scene between the king and Tudor, in which the latter reveals the story of his love. The king promises to plead Tudor's cause.

Act V

The opening and conclusion of this act are taken up with the victory of Henry in politics; the middle with his victory in love.

Henry the Fifth's character in Orrery's play is not on the whole remarkable, and yet it may properly serve as an instance of a hero. It is not conspicuous; still it possesses the usual traits of its kind, which in brief are excellence in war and love, and it does not admit any elements not also found in other heroic plays.

APPENDIX C

BURLESQUE OF THE HEROIC PLAY

The following scene taken from [Arrowsmith's] "Reformation, a Comedy." 1673. Act IV, Sc. 1, is one of the most comprehensive satires on rhymed tragedy. The scene is Italy, the characters Italian except Tutor, an Englishman, who is questioned as to the manner of dramatic composition in his country, and thus gives instructions how to write an heroic play.

"*Tut.* Faith — well, for an essay. I guess the Gentlemans but a beginner. I myself —

Pis. Now he's in. (*Aside.*)

Tut. Writ with the fame much success at first, 'twas industry and much converse that made me ripe; I tell you Gentlemen, when I first attemped this way, I understood no more of Poetry than one of you.

Ped. This is strange impudence. } *Aside.*
Ant. 'Tis nothing yet. }

Tut. There are many pretenders but you see how few succeed; and bating two or three of this nation as *Tasso*, *Ariosto* and *Guarini*, that write indifferently well, the rest must not be named for *Poesy:* we have some three or four, as *Fletcher*, *Johnson*, *Shakespear*, *Davenant*, that have scribled themselves into the bulk of follies and are admired to, but ne'er knew the laws of heroick or dramatick poesy, nor faith to write true English neither.

Ant. 'Tis very much I hope sir your heroick play goes on.

Tut. As fast as a piece of that exactness can. I'le only leave a pattern to the world for the succeeding ages and have done.

Ped. Oh Sir you'l wrong the world.

Tut. No faith Sir I grow weary of applause.

Ant. Will you give me leave to ask the way for others to attain to your perfection?

Tut. I will not say but that it may be done, but trust me you'l find it hard Gentlemen, and since you are my friends I'le tell you.

Ped. You will oblige us Sir.

Tut. First I speak of Tragedy, which, let the world say what it will and doat on little things, I scrible now and then, as good faith they doe Gentlemen strangely; you shall have them — but I don't love to praise myself. Tragedy I say's my Masterpiece.

Ant. Everything you do seems so.

Tut. Nay, nay, pray forbear Gentlemen. — To go on: I take a subject, as suppose the Siege of *Candy*, or the conquest of *Flanders*, and by the way Sir let it alwayes be some warlike action; you can't imagine what a grace a Drum and Trumpet give a Play. Then Sir I take you some three or four or half a dozen Kings, but most commonly two or three serve my turn, not a farthing matter whether they lived within a hundred years of one another, not a farthing Gentlemen, I have tryed it, and let the Play be what it will, the Characters are still the same.

Pis. Trust me Sir, this is a secret of your art.

Tut. As Sir you must alwayes have two Ladies in Love with one man, or two men in love with one woman; if you make them the Father and the Son or two Brothers, or two Friends, 'twill do the better. There you know is opportunity for love and honour and Fighting, and all that.

Ped. Very well Sir.

Tut. Then Sir you must have a Hero that shall fight with all the world; yes i' gad, and beat them too, and half the gods into the bargain if occassion serves.

Ant. This method must needs take.

Tut. And does Sir. But give me leave and mark it for

infallible, in all you write reflect upon religion and the Clergy; you can't imagine how it tickles, you shall have the Gallants get those verses all by heart, and fill their letters with them to their Country friends; believe me this one piece of art has set off many an indifferent Play, and but you are my friends —

Ant. You honour us.

Tut. Last of all, be sure to raise a dancing singing ghost or two, court the Players for half a dozen new scenes and fine cloaths (for take me if there ben't much in that too) put your story into rime, and kill enough at the end of the Play, and *Probatum est* your business is done for Tragedy."

One of the best-known heroic plays was Settle's "Empress of Morocco." A quotation, chiefly concerned with imagery, from the Prologue to T. Duffet's burlesque of the same name, 1674, follows. There are other instances of a parody of a play bearing the same title as the original. Frequently, however, the title itself suggests both source and character, as "Mock Tempest" and "Psyche Debauch'd."

"As when some dogrel-monger raises
Up Muse, to flatter Doxies praises,
He talks of Gems and Paradises,
Perfumes and Arabian Spices:
Making up Phantastick Posies
Of Eye-lids, Fore-heads, Cheeks and Noses,
Calling them Lillies, Pinks and Roses.
Teeth Orient Pearl, Coral Lips are,
Neck's Alablaster and Marble Hips are;
Prating of Diamonds, Saphyrs, Rubies,
What a Pudder's with these Boobies?
Dim Eyes are Stars, and Red hairs Guinnies:
And thus described by these Ninnies,

As they sit scribling on Ale-Benches,
Are homely dowdy Country Wenches.
So when this Plot quite purg'd of Ale is,
In naked truth but a plain Tale is;
And in such dress we mean to shew it,
In spight of our damn'd Fustian Poet,
Who has disguis'd it with dull Hist'ris,
Worse than his Brethren e're did Mistress."

The large quantity of contemporary allusions and references and the presence of burlesque are an undeniable proof of the popularity of the heroic play. The last line of the extract below, from the epilogue to the same farce, contains a very plausible generalization.

"Be to this joy thus kind you'l rouse up yet,
Much better Farce, one more Heroick Puppet;
When little Worm is prais'd it will so brag o't,
That 'twill set Tail on end of bigger Maggot;
Since with success great Bard's grow proud and resty,
To get good Plays be kind to bad Travesty."

But in the Restoration there arose four kinds of dramatic entertainment: comedy of manners, heroic play, opera, and travesty. The name of D'Avenant is intimately associated with the beginnings of all of them, comedy only excepted. For it is said that the last act of the "Playhouse to be Let," staged probably in 1664, and printed in 1673, is "the earliest burlesque dramatic piece in the English language" (Dramatic Works of Sir William D'Avenant, edited by James Maidment and W. H. Logan, 1872, iv. 6). It is to be noted that travesty did not arise until the Golden Age of the English drama had passed, and it was not successful, in its early stages at least, in begetting good plays.

APPENDIX D

A LIST OF PLAYS WRITTEN PARTLY OR WHOLLY IN HEROIC VERSE, TOGETHER WITH REPRESENTATIVE REFERENCES. 1656–1703.

NOTE. — The reference to Dibdin is to "History of the Stage"; to Downes, Knight's edition of "Roscius Anglicanus"; to Garnett, "Age of Dryden"; to Gosse, "Seventeenth Century Studies"; to Jacob, "Poetical Register"; to Langbaine and Gildon, the latter's additions to the former's work; to Noel, the Introduction to Otway in the Mermaid series; to Saintsbury, the "Life of Dryden"; to Scott, the first volume of the Scott-Saintsbury edition of Dryden. The reference to Baker is to the first edition of "Companion to the Play-house," whereas Biog. Dram. is an abbreviation for "Biographica Dramatica," an enlarged and altered edition of the same work. The other references are sufficiently self-explanatory.

Unless otherwise stated, it is to be understood that a play was acted and published the same year.

ALCIBIADES. BY THOMAS OTWAY. 1675.

Baker.
Dibdin. i. 100.
Downes. p. 36.
Garnett. p. 102.
Genest. i. 177 (D. G. 1675).
Gosse. pp. 274, 277.

Jacob. i. 195.
Langbaine. p. 396.
Noel. p. xi.
Ward. i. 413.

ALMANZOR AND ALMAHIDE; OR, THE CONQUEST OF GRANADA BY THE SPANIARDS. IN TWO PARTS. BY JOHN DRYDEN. 1672. First part acted 1669; second part acted 1670.

Biog. Dram.
Garnett. pp. 85, 85.
Genest. i. 101, 102 (T. R. 1670).
Jacob. i. 81.
Langbaine. p. 157.
Saintsbury. p. 46.
Scott. p. 95.
Ward. iii. 360.

ALTEMIRA. BY LORD ORRERY (ROGER BOYLE). 1702.

Anon. Life of Betterton. p. 127.
Biog. Dram.
Genest. i. 260 (L. I. F. 1702).
Jacob. i. 305.
Ward. iii. 344.

AMAZON QUEEN; OR, THE AMOURS OF THALESTRIS TO ALEXANDER THE GREAT. BY JOHN WESTON. 1667. Never acted.

Baker.
Langbaine. p. 510.
Langbaine and Gildon. p. 147.

ANTONY AND CLEOPATRA. BY SIR CHARLES SEDLEY. 1677.

Anon. Life of Betterton. p. 94.
Genest. i. 208 (D. G. 1677).
Langbaine. p. 487.
Ward. iii. 447.

AURENG-ZEBE. BY JOHN DRYDEN. 1676.

Garnett. p. 87.
Genest. i. 174 (T. R. 1675).
Langbaine. p. 156.
Saintsbury. p. 56.
Scott. p. 175.
Ward. i. 370.

BLACK PRINCE. BY LORD ORRERY (ROGER BOYLE). 1669. Acted 1667.

Genest. i. 70 (T. R. 1667).
Langbaine. p. 27.
Pepys' Diary. 19 Oct., 1667; 23 Oct., 1667; 1 April, 1668.
Ward. iii. 343.

BOADICEA, QUEEN OF GREAT BRITAIN. BY CHARLES HOPKINS. 1697.

Anon. Life of Betterton. p. 125.
Downes. p. 44.
Genest. ii. 118 (L. I. F. 1697).
Jacob. p. 141.
Langbaine and Gildon. p. 74.

CALIGULA. BY JOHN CROWNE. 1698.

Garnett. p. 115.
Genest. ii. 143 (D. L. 1698).
Ward. i. 403.

CAMBYSES, KING OF PERSIA. BY ELKANAH SETTLE. 1671. Acted 1667.

Anon. Life of Betterton. p. 81.
Dibdin. iv. 188.
Downes. p. 27.
Genest. i. 73 (L. I. F. 1667).
Langbaine. p. 440.
Prologue. See play.
Scott. p. 155 (foot-note).
Ward. iii. 396.

CHARLES VIII OF FRANCE; OR, THE INVASION OF NAPLES BY THE FRENCH, HISTORY OF. BY JOHN CROWNE. 1672. Acted 1671.

Dibdin. iv. 164.
Downes. p. 32.
Genest. i. 124 (D. G. 1671).
Langbaine. p. 92.
Ward. iii. 400.

COMICAL REVENGE; OR, LOVE IN A TUB. BY SIR GEORGE ETHEREDGE. 1664.

Anon. Life of Betterton, p. 77.
Baker.
Evelyn's Diary. 27 April, 1664.
Downes. p. 24.

Genest. i. 54 (L. I. F. 1664).
Gosse. pp. 235, 236, 239, 242.
Langbaine. p. 187.
Pepys' Diary. Oct. 29–31, 1666.
Ward. iii. 444.

CONQUEST OF CHINA BY THE TARTARS. BY ELKANAH SETTLE. 1676. Acted 1674.

Dibdin. iv. 188.
Downes. p. 35.
Genest. i. 170 (D. G. 1674).
Langbaine. p. 440.
Ward. iii. 393.

CONSPIRACY; OR, THE CHANGE OF GOVERNMENT. BY W. WHITAKER. 1680.

Genest. i. 280 (D. G. 1680).
Langbaine. p. 511.

DESTRUCTION OF JERUSALEM BY TITUS VESPASIAN. IN TWO PARTS. BY JOHN CROWNE. 1677.

Dibdin. iv. 164.
Genest. i. 204 (T. R. 1677).
Langbaine. pp. 95, 529.
Ward. iii. 400.

DESTRUCTION OF TROY. BY JOHN BANKES. 1679. Acted 1678.

Baker.
Dibdin. iv. 197.
Downes. p. 37.
Genest. i. 241 (D. G. 1678).
Langbaine. p. 7.

DON CARLOS, PRINCE OF SPAIN. BY THOMAS OTWAY. 1676.

Anon. Life of Betterton. p. 93.
Garnett. p. 102.
Dibdin. iv. 101.
Downes. p. 36.
Genest. i. 190 (D. G. 1676).
Gosse. pp. 279, 281.
Langbaine. p. 398.
Noel. p. 2.
Scott. p. 163.
Ward. iii. 414.

DOUBLE DISTRESS. BY MRS. MARY PIX. 1701.

Biog. Dram.
Dibdin. iv. 344.
Genest. i. 240 (L. I. F. 1701).
Jacob. i. 204.

EDGAR; OR, THE ENGLISH MONARCH. BY THOMAS RYMER. 1678. Never acted.

Baker.
Dibdin. iv. 124.
Genest. i. 223.
Langbaine. p. 434.

EMPRESS OF MOROCCO. BY ELKANAH SETTLE. 1673. Acted 1671.

Garnett. p. 118.
Genest. i. 154 (D. G. 1673).
Jacob. i. 220.
Johnson. Life of Dryden.
Langbaine. p. 440.

Scott. p. 158.
Ward. iii. 396.

ENGLISH PRINCESS; OR, DEATH OF RICHARD III.
BY J. CARYL (?). 1667.

Anon. Life of Betterton. p. 82.
Downes. p. 27.
Genest. i. 73 (L. I. F. 1667).
Pepys' Diary. March 7, 1666–1667.

FATAL JEALOUSIE. BY NEVIL PAYNE (?). 1673.
Acted 1672.

Biog. Dram.
Downes. p. 33.
Genest. i. 144 (D. G. 1672).
Langbaine. p. 531.

GLORIANA; OR, THE COURT OF AUGUSTUS CÆSAR.
BY NATHANIEL LEE. 1676.

Baker.
Dibden. iv. 185.
Genest. i. 185 (T. R. 1676).
Langbaine. p. 322.

GREAT FAVORITE; OR, THE DUKE OF LERMA. BY SIR
ROBERT HOWARD. 1668.

Genest. i. 80 (T. R. 1668).
Langbaine. p. 276.
Pepys' Diary. Jan. 11, 1667; Jan. 20, 1667; April 18, 1668.
Ward. iii. 394.

King Henry V; History of. By Lord Orrery (Roger Boyle). 1667. Acted 1664.

Downes. p. 27.
Genest. i. 53 (L. I. F. 1664).
Langbaine. p. 28.
Pepys' Diary. Aug. 10, 1664; Aug. 13, 1664; Aug. 17, 1664; Sept. 28, 1664; Dec. 28, 1666; Feb. 13, 1666-1667; Oct. 19, 1667; July 6, 1668.
Ward. iii. 342.

Henry the Third of France Stabb'd by a Fryer with the Fall of the Guise. By Thomas Shipman. 1678.

Genest. i. 229 (T. R. 1678).
Langbaine. p. 473.

Herod and Mariamne. By Samuel Pordage. 1673.

Genest. i. 171 (D. G. 1674).
Langbaine. p. 406.

Herod the Great. By Lord Orrery (Roger Boyle). 1694. Never acted.

Genest. i. 131.
Ward. iii. 344.

Ibrahim, the Illustrious Bassa. By Elkanah Settle. 1677. Acted 1676.

Genest. i. 187 (D. G. 1676).
Langbaine. p. 441.
Pepys' Diary. June 19, 1668.
Ward. iii. 395.

Indian Emperor; or, Conquest of Mexico. By John Dryden. 1667. Acted 1665.

Dibdin. iv. 157.
Garnett. pp. 76–77.
Genest. i. (T. R. 1665).
Langbaine. p. 165.
Pepys' Diary. Jan. 15, 1666–1667; Aug. 22, 1667; Oct. 28, 1667; Nov. 11, 1667; Jan. 14, 1667–1668; Mar. 28, 1668; April 21, 1668.
Saintsbury. p. 42.
Scott. p. 71.
Ward. iii. 349.

Indian Queen. By Sir Robert Howard and John Dryden. 1665. Acted 1664.

Evelyn's Diary. Feb. 5, 1664.
Genest. i. 57 (T. R. 1665).
Langbaine. p. 276.
Pepys' Diary. Jan. 27, 1663–1664; June 27, 1668.
Saintsbury. p. 42.
Scott. p. 69.
Ward. iii. 348.

Love's Triumph; or, the Royal Union. By Ed. Cooke. 1678.

Baker.
Langbaine. p. 71.
Ward. iii. 295.

King Saul, Tragedy of. By Rev. Joseph Trapp (?). 1703. Never acted.

Genest. x. 151.

MARCELIA, OR THE TREACHEROUS FRIEND. BY MRS. FRANCIS BOOTHBY. 1670. Acted 1669.

Genest. i. 97 (T. R. 1669).

MARRIAGE-A-LA-MODE. BY JOHN DRYDEN. 1673.

Dibdin. iv. p. 166.
Genest. i. 133 (T. R. 1672).
Langbaine. p. 166.
Saintsbury. p. 54.
Scott. p. 122.
Ward. iii. 366, 367.

MUSTAPHA, SON OF SOLYMAN THE MAGNIFICENT. BY LORD ORRERY (ROGER BOYLE). 1668. Acted 1665.

Downes. p. 25.
Evelyn's Diary. Sept. 18, 1666.
Genest. i. 61.
Langbaine. p. 28.
Pepys' Diary. April 3, 1665; Jan. 5, 1666–1667; Sept. 3, 1667.
Ward. iii. 343.

NERO, EMPEROR OF ROME; HIS TRAGEDY. BY NATHANIEL LEE. 1675.

Genest. i. 172 (T. R. 1675).
Gosse. p. 277.
Langbaine. p. 324.
Ward. iii. 408.

RIVAL KINGS; OR, THE LOVES OF OROONDATES AND STATIRA. BY JOHN BANKES. 1677.

Baker.
Dibdin. iv. 197.

Genest. i. 200 (T. R. 1677).
Langbaine. p. 8.

RIVAL LADIES. BY JOHN DRYDEN. 1664. Acted 1663.

Genest. i. 50 (T. R. 1664).
Langbaine. p. 167.
Pepys' Diary. July 18, 1666; Aug. 2, 1666; Aug. 4, 1664.
Saintsbury. p. 42.
Scott. pp. 68, 69.
Ward. iii. 347.

RIVAL SISTERS; OR, THE VIOLENCE OF LOVE. BY ROBERT GOULD. 1696.

Baker.
Genest. ii. 75 (D. G. 1696).
Jacob. i. 119.
Langbaine and Gildon. p. 65.

SACRIFICE. BY SIR FRANCIS FANE. 1686. Never acted.

Genest. x. 147.
Langbaine. p. 189.

SECRET LOVE; OR, THE MAIDEN QUEEN. BY JOHN DRYDEN. 1668.

Dibdin. iv. 157.
Langbaine. p. 169.

Pepys' Diary. Jan. 19, 1666–1667; Mar. 25, 1666–1667; Aug. 23, 1667; Jan. 24, 1667–1668; May 24, 1667.
Saintsbury. p. 43.
Scott. p. 89.
Ward. iii. 350.

Siege of Babylon. By Samuel Pordage. 1678.
Acted 1677.

Anon. Life of Betterton. p. 95.
Genest. i. 213 (D. G. 1677).
Langbaine. p. 406.

Siege of Memphis; or, the Ambitious Queen.
By Thomas Durfey. 1676.

Dibdin. iv. 180.
Genest. iv. 183 (T. R. 1676).
Langbaine. p. 183.

Siege of Rhodes. By Sir William D'Avenant.
1656.

Downes. p. 20.
Evelyn's Diary. Jan. 9, 1662.
Genest. i. 37 (L. I. F. 1661).
Knight. (pref. to Downes) pp. xv–xxii.
Langbaine. p. 110.

Pepys' Diary. June 2, 1661; Nov. 15, 1661; May 19, 1662; Dec. 27, 1662; Sept. 23, 1664; Oct. 1, 1665; Jan. 23, 1666; Dec. 19, 1668.
Ward. iii. 328.

Sophonisba; or, Hannibal's Overthrow. By
Nathaniel Lee. 1676.

Dibdin. iv. 185.
Genest. i. 183 (T. R. 1676).
Langbaine. p. 325.
Ward. iii. 408–409.

State of Innocence; and, Fall of Man. By John Dryden. 1674. Never acted.

Dibdin. iii. 168.
Jacob. i. 81.
Genest. i. 180.
Langbaine. p. 172.
Scott. p. 140.

Tryphon. By Lord Orrery (Roger Boyle). 1668.

Genest. i. 87. ("Never acted.")
Langbaine. p. 28. ("Acted.")
Ward. iii. 344.

Tyrannic Love; or, the Virgin Martyr. By John Dryden. 1670. Acted 1669.

Biog. Dram. iii.
Dibdin. iv. 163.
Garnett. p. 84.
Genest. i. 94 (T. R. 1669).
Hogarth. i. 119.
Jacob. i. 82.
Johnson. Life of Dryden.
Langbaine. p. 173.
Langbaine and Gildon. p. 47.
Saintsbury. p. 44.
Scott. p. 94.

Vestal Virgin; or, the Roman Ladies. By Sir Robert Howard. 1665.

Genest. i. 56 (D. G. 1665).
Langbaine. p. 277.

INDEX